THE NORTH AMERICAN

HUNTER'S HANDBOOK

THE NORTH AMERICAN

HUNTER'S HANDBOOK

Marcus Schneck

RUNNING PRESS
PHILADELPHIA, PENNSYLVANIA

DEDICATION

To Dad, who gave me my first gun
and my love of the outdoors.

A QUINTET BOOK

Text copyright © 1991 Quintet Publishing
Limited. All rights reserved under the Pan
American and International Copyright
Convention.
First published in the United States of America in
1991 by Running Press Book Publishers

9 8 7 6 5 4 3 2 1
Digit on the right indicates the
number of this printing

Library of Congress Cataloging-in-Publication
Number 90-50833

ISBN 0-89471-973-4

This book was designed and produced by
Quintet Publishing Limited London

Creative Director: Terry Jeavons
Art Director: Helen Beauvais
Designer: Helen Beauvais
Project Editor: Sally Harper
Editor: Susan Ward

Typeset in Great Britain by
Central Southern Typesetters, Eastbourne
Manufactured in Hong Kong by
Regent Publishing Services Limited
Printed in Hong Kong by
Leefung-Asco Printers Limited

This book may be ordered by mail from the
publisher. Please add $2.50 for postage and
handling.
But try your bookstore first!
Running Press Book Publishers
125 South Twenty-second Street
Philadelphia, Pennsylvania 19103

CONTENTS

Introduction

to its den. The buck and I relaxed our guard.

A pair of mourning doves whizzed by overhead. They were out of sight almost as soon as I realized they were there.

The deer was very close now, maybe 15 yards away. Although well within range, it still had not taken enough notice of me to cause it concern. The wind was blowing in my direction, carrying my scent away from the animal.

My muscles tensed in the familiar response that often takes hold when such a magnificent animal comes so close, a tension that brings the senses to a peak and blots out everything uninvolved in my concentration on the animal. Then the deer was gone, taking the final step into the cornfield and out of sight just as the final bit of daylight faded.

It was a perfect evening of hunting, even though not a shot had been fired. It wasn't deer

With the briefcase stowed in the trunk and my suit flung over the back seat, I headed out across the field in my camouflage. A deep red sun was edging closer to the horizon much faster than I would have preferred. It was always like this when I could grab an hour or two for hunting after work. Not nearly enough time, but infinitely better than none.

I moved quickly but cautiously to the spot at the edge of the cornfield I had chosen previously: near a slight depression in the earth that acted like a funnel for all game coming to the corn for its nightly feast. With my back to the field, I looked out over a spread of weeds that covered the 50 yards or so to the edge of the forest. A trampled game trail led from the forest to the corn. If I stood motionless, my camouflage would blend into the cornfield and render me almost invisible to the animals coming up that trail.

Only a few minutes had passed – just enough time to savor the ongoing chill of a late September night – before a whitetail deer emerged at the edge of the forest. A careful glance through the binoculars confirmed that it was a buck, a nice eight-pointer.

The deer appeared not to notice me at all as it started slowly in my direction, munching on some lush clovers here and there. Occasionally it would come to a complete stop, its ears erect and with all of its considerable attention focused squarely upon me. Satisfied, after staring at my motionless form for a minute or two, he would return to his eating/walking manner, moving toward the corn.

Something crashed through a section of taller weeds to my left. Both the buck and I jerked our heads to discern what was causing the ruckus. A plump groundhog stood on its hind legs at the mound of dirt and stones marking the entrance

ABOVE: Although the location and appearance varies greatly, deer camp is a highlight of the year for any hunter. This is a coastal deer camp in the southern United States.

BELOW: For many hunters, the joy of the sport is enhanced by spending the time outdoors with a faithful canine companion. With the proper training, breeds like the Irish setter grow into fine bird dogs.

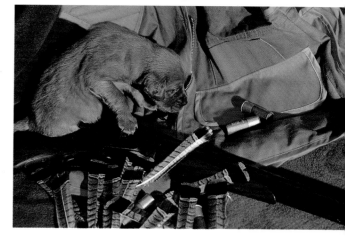

RIGHT: An Arkansas archer heads home with his trophy over his shoulder.

BELOW: Alone in the untamed, clean and pure wilderness, it almost doesn't matter if the hunt ends in a kill. There are rewards here beyond meat for the table and trophy for the wall.

hunters I know truly search. If they manage to put some game in the bag along the way, so much the better.

The anti-hunters across the continent, who see hunters as nothing more than neanderthals with some serious personality defects, might be surprised by this. But, despite that viewpoint, the best hunters I know are also the most dedicated conservationists. They are the men and women whom I expect to make a real difference in the crucial struggle for the salvation of our planet.

The fact that they happen to carry a gun – or a bow and arrows – into the fields and forests at certain times during the year only serves to further convince me. They are the members of the human race who have come closest to the earth and its elemental and interconnecting natural forces. These people base their thoughts and convictions on more than a television or movie version of the natural world. They've been there. They appreciate what's involved in putting meat on the table. They know the meat in the supermarket starts out as a living, breathing animal that must be sacrificed for man to eat.

These are the people I want to trust with the future of this planet. Hunting has not perverted their characters. It has strengthened their understanding, their knowledge and their feelings.

All this is not to say that hunting doesn't have its darker side. That can't be denied. We have not yet rid ourselves of that minority who are in it for the kill, who are not satisfied with a day that doesn't end with a filled game bag.

We come from a tradition that admittedly has measured the success of the hunt by the size of the kill. But our hunting heritage harkens back

season; the start of archery season for deer was still a day or two away. It *was* dove season, but the only members of that species I had seen were well out of range before I could raise the shotgun. Nevertheless, it was the essence of the sport we call hunting. The pull of the trigger, the shot at the animal, is only the climax. The tasty meal that might be prepared with bagged game is only the gravy atop everything else – the sights, the sounds, the smells – that really makes up the experience. It is those elements for which most

to the most noble of survival instincts and tracking skills that pitted man against beast on a common level. It includes a closeness and dedication to the land and its creatures that is largely unmatched by other pursuits. But it also has a less attractive history; market hunters who slaughtered wagonloads of passenger pigeons for a couple cents a pound or butchered entire prairies of bison for nothing more than the animals' tongues and hides. There were the hawk shooters who lay in ambush along the birds' annual migration route, picking off the birds until the "hunters" stood in knee-deep piles – this for no other reason than the excitement of the kill.

It's important for all of us to remember both sides of our heritage. The kill-hungry will be with us for years to come, but in ever-decreasing numbers. The sport of hunting is changing. It must, in response to a changing world and a changing environment. The sport is also adapting

in another way. With each passing year the equipment available seems to advance to a new level of state-of-the-art. New materials like Gore-Tex, Thinsulate and Kevlar have transformed many traditional pieces of gear.

Individuals across the country are devoting themselves to learning the most intimate secrets of game animals' lives, resulting in an ever greater selection of lures, baits, calls, decoys and the like. Annual hunting gear catalogs grow thicker with each publication, burgeoning with tempting items to further enhance our enjoyment of the sport.

While the sheer number of products is growing at an unbelievable rate and shows no evidence of slowing down, most new equipment tends to fall into a few general categories that have been with

us almost since the first hunters pursued their quarry. These are weapons, ammunition and accouterments; the knife, apparel and footwear; and general accessories.

Hunting weapons are of four major types: shotgun, rifle, muzzleloader and bow. Each has almost infinite variety of design; here I can explain only the basic options for each. Many fine books have been written with a specialized focus on firearms, or on archery equipment, and these might be sought out for greater detail. Most specialist sporting goods shops – *not* sporting goods departments in department stores – employ people who are very knowledgable about the equipment they sell and are quite willing to share that information with hunters.

ABOVE LEFT: A wildlife biologist uses telemetry to monitor the movements of the bobcats he is studying. Radio telemetry has allowed biologists to gain a great deal of information in a relatively short time about many species.

ABOVE RIGHT: Radio telemetry has played a major role in research of animals, both game and non-game, across the country.

Shotguns

The modern shotgun is generally one of five designs:

● Single-barrel break action: the most inexpensive and simplest design. This is often a boy's first gun, probably in the 20-gauge model (gauges will be explained shortly). To load and expel shells the gun is simply "cracked" at the end of the barrel.

● Double-barrel break action is available as either side-by-side, which carries the two barrels next to each other, or over-and-under, which places one atop of the other. The two barrels are generally "choked" (explained shortly) differently. Most have two triggers, allowing the hunter to make the choice of which barrel to fire first. Others have a single trigger, which fires the more open barrel first. The most expensive doubles offer a single selective trigger that allows the hunter to choose which barrel will fire first through the movement of an additional button near the safety catch. As with the single-barrel shotgun, loading and expelling shells is accomplished by "cracking" the gun open.

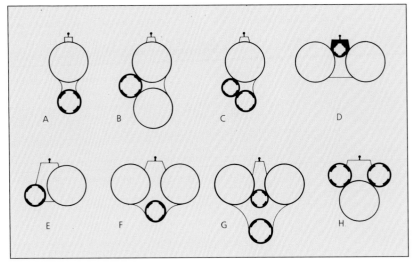

COMBINATION GUN TYPES
A. Over-and-under with shotgun on top and rifle under.
B. Over-and-under shotgun with rifle at side.
C. Shotgun at top, rifles under and at side.
D. Rifle on top, side-by-side shotgun.
E. Side-by-side rifle and shotgun.
F. Side-by-side shotgun with rifle under.
G. Side-by-side shotgun with two rifles under.
H. Side-by-side double rifle with shotgun under.

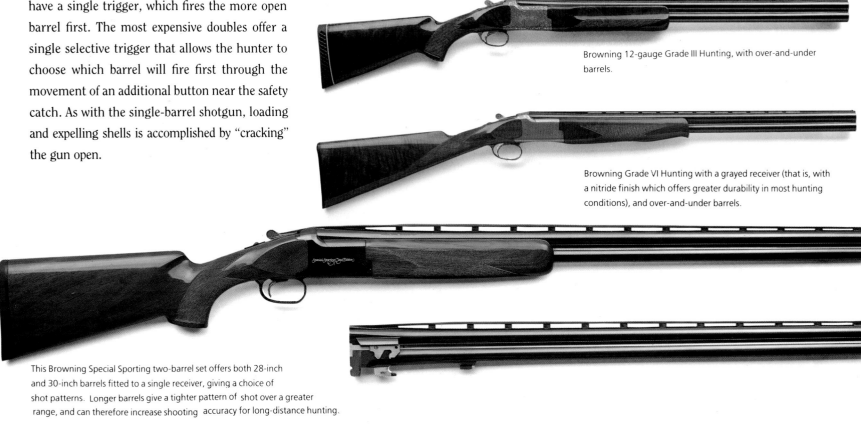

BREAK ACTION SHOTGUNS

Browning 12-gauge Grade III Hunting, with over-and-under barrels.

Browning Grade VI Hunting with a grayed receiver (that is, with a nitride finish which offers greater durability in most hunting conditions), and over-and-under barrels.

This Browning Special Sporting two-barrel set offers both 28-inch and 30-inch barrels fitted to a single receiver, giving a choice of shot patterns. Longer barrels give a tighter pattern of shot over a greater range, and can therefore increase shooting accuracy for long-distance hunting.

RIGHT: These pump-action shotguns represent a range of the bore sizes available. (As gauge increases, the size of the bore decreases.) The most common gauges are 12 and 20, but gauges range from as small as 410 to as large as 10.

PUMP-ACTION SHOTGUNS

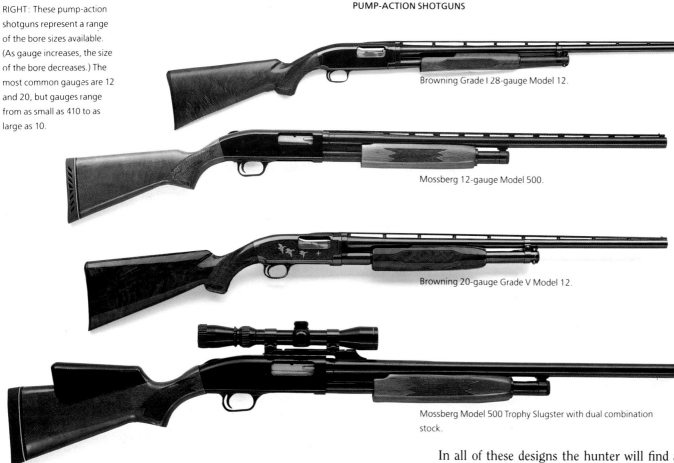

Browning Grade I 28-gauge Model 12.

Mossberg 12-gauge Model 500.

Browning 20-gauge Grade V Model 12.

Mossberg Model 500 Trophy Slugster with dual combination stock.

BORE DIAMETERS OF SHOTGUN GAUGES

10-gauge — .775 inch

12-gauge — .730 inch

16-gauge — .670 inch

20-gauge — .615 inch

28-gauge — .550 inch

410-gauge — .410 inch

● Pump-action shotguns are the most popular today, offering a capacity of three or more shells loaded at a time and moved into the firing position by the "pumping" backwards of the fore-end. The fired shell is expelled through the port and the new shell is ready to fire all in one smooth motion.

● Autoloaders are simply pump-action shotguns that require no manual operation after each shot to load the next into the firing position. This is done automatically, either gas-operated or recoil-operated.

● Bolt-action shotguns are few and far between. They offer none of the advantages of any of the other models, but they are very inexpensive.

In all of these designs the hunter will find a half-dozen gauge sizes available, ranging from 10 to 410. This system was devised long ago to quantify the number of lead balls that would fit into the bore as a measure based on one pound. For example, a 12-gauge would hold a ball that weighed 1/12th of a pound and the 20-gauge would hold a ball that weighed 1/20th of a pound. For more practical purposes it is necessary to remember only that the lower the number the more powerful the shotgun. It also is generally a heavier weapon to carry.

The 12-gauge is the top all-round shotgun today. Loaded with different shells, it is effective on everything from small game to deer.

No.	9	8½	8	7½	6	5	4	2	1	BB
SHOT SIZES Diameter in inches	.08	.085	.09	.095	.11	.12	.13	.15	.16	.18

BUCKSHOT Diameter in inches	No. 4	No. 3	No. 2	No. 1	No. 0	No. 00
	.24	.25	.27	.30	.32	.33

SHOT PELLETS PER OUNCE (Approximate)

LEAD				STEEL	
Size	Pellets	Size	Pellets	Size	Pellets
BB	60	6	225	BB	72
2	87	7½	350	1	103
4	135	8	410	2	125
5	170	9	585	4	192

THE SHOTSHELL SELECTOR
Lead Shot Unless Indicated "Steel"

	Type of Shell	Size
DUCKS	Magnum or High power	4, 5, 6 / Steel 2, 4
GEESE	Magnum or High power	BB, 2, 4 / Steel BB, 1, 2
PHEASANTS	Field load or high power	5, 6, 7½
QUAIL	High power or field load	7½, 8, 9
RUFFED GROUSE & CHUKARS	High power or field load	5, 6, 7½, 8
DOVES & PIGEONS	High power or field load	6, 7½, 8, 9
RABBITS	High power or field load	4, 5, 6, 7½
WOODCOCK, SNIPE, RAIL	Field load	7½, 8, 9
SQUIRRELS	High power or field load	4, 5, 6
WILD TURKEY	Magnum or high power	BB, 2, 4, 5, 6
CROWS	High power or field load	5, 6, 7½
FOX	Magnum or high power	BB, 2, 4

Courtesy of Federal Cartridge

The shotgun barrel carries two other design factors which are equally important considerations: length and choke. Longer barrels tend to give a tighter pattern of shot over a greater range, although modern shotgun shells are designed to give much the same effect.

Choke is the measure of the constriction of the barrel and works like the nozzle of a hose. Tighten the nozzle and the water streams out in a tighter pattern. Shotgun chokes range from full – which gives the tightest pattern – to skeet cylinder, which offers the widest pattern. In between we find improved, modified, quarter, open, improved cylinder and skeet.

BELOW: Winchester Classic 12-gauge shotgun, showing the break action at work.

CHOKE TUBES FOR SHOTGUNS

Choke tubes are used to change a gun's capability to suit different game and conditions. These are fitted into the muzzle to change the choke. The tubes on the left are compatible with both lead and steel shot. The four choke tubes shown at top right are for use with steel shot only, while the group of six tubes shown below right are lead compatible. Although lead shot is used for most hunting, steel shot should be used in wetland and aquatic environments: spent lead may be ingested by waterfowl then become poisonous in their systems. Some shotguns are sold with a range of choke tubes to suit that weapon.

RIGHT: Three types of rifled slugs; most states allow the use of such solid slugs by deer hunters.

FAR RIGHT: Some magnum shells have longer cases to hold even more shot and powder. Never attempt to shoot a long-cased magnum shell in a gun chambered for standard shells, as the chamber will be too short to accommodate a magnum load. (The proper shell length is usually engraved on the barrel.)

Into the shotgun, the hunter places the shells. These are available in quite a variety of shot sizes and powder loads. The exact combination chosen will depend on game being sought and on personal preference. Shot sizes range from the small No. 9s, in which each pellet is approximately .08 of an inch in diameter, to BBs, in which each pellet is about .18 of an inch in diameter. The larger the number, the smaller the shot size. With the No. 9s there are almost 600 pellets to an ounce, while there are about 50 of the BBs in an ounce.

Smaller shot sizes are used for smaller game and quarry that has been shown to go down relatively easily. For example, No. 9 is fine for quail, dove and woodcock, but for the larger and tougher pheasant No. 5 or 6 is the accepted size. BB or No. 2 is recommended for turkey.

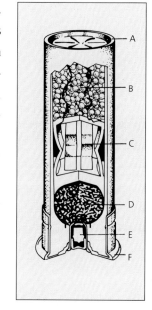

PARTS OF A SHOTSHELL
A modern shotshell consists of six main parts: (A) a one-piece body, incorporating top crimp and base wad; (B) shot charge; (C) a one-piece wad to provide a sealed chamber over the powder and protect the shot; (D) ball powder; (E) primer; and (F) brass head.

In addition, there is buckshot – which, as the name implies, is intended for use on deer. This ranges from the smallest, No. 4, through to the largest, No. 00.

Most hunting is done with shot made of lead, which is cheap and soft enough to prevent damage to the shotgun barrel in firing. However, in wetland and aquatic environments, the spent lead is often ingested by waterfowl and can become poisonous in their systems. Therefore, steel shot should be used when hunting in or near these environments, and is always the best choice for the conservation-minded waterfowler.

The second component of every shell is the powder that has been loaded into it. The amount is expressed in drams equivalent, a somewhat antiquated measurement, which compares the load in power and velocity to drams of black powder. For the average hunter, however, it is sufficient to know that the more powder contained in the shot, the greater the force and velocity of the shot.

Also available are magnum shells, which carry more shot and powder than standard loads. They have a longer effective range and additional power against tougher game like geese or turkeys.

Rifles

These are available in four basic variations:

● Bolt action, which functions similarly to the bolt action of a shotgun. It is the simplest design, and the easiest to maintain and repair in the field. It can be single shot or multi-shot, employing a clip or a magazine of bullets which is chambered into the firing position.

● Lever action, which is the design seen most often in the rifles employed by cowboys and Indians in western movies. A downward then upward movement of the lever ejects the spent cartridge and moves another from the magazine into firing position. The lever action sacrifices a bit of accuracy to offer faster loading than the bolt action. It is more difficult to repair a minor problem out in the field when using a lever action rifle.

● Pump action, which functions like the pump-action shotgun. It is even faster than the lever action, but also suffers a loss of accuracy. Problems encountered in the field with a pump action will more than likely bring the day's hunting to a close unless a spare gun is available.

● Semi-automatic or autoloading, which are rifle versions of the shotgun autoloaders. These are the least accurate and most troublesome of all rifles.

All actions are available in a large array of caliber, which is the diameter of the bore of the gun. Calibers range from the narrow bore .17 and .22 calibers, for very small game like varmints and squirrels, to the most powerful .458 and .460 calibers, for the largest and sturdiest animals.

SOME BASIC RIFLE ACTIONS

Semi-automatic: the Browning Grade I BAR is a semi-automatic centerfire rifle. This is a no sights model, which is relatively rare.

Semi-automatic: the Browning BAR Magnum is also a semi-automatic rifle, but is designed to take magnum loads.

Bolt action: this Browning A-Bolt Medallion is a bolt action centerfire rifle, shown here in the left-hand version (an option offered by some manufacturers).

Lever action: a lever action rifle, the Browning Deluxe Grade model 53 is a modern reproduction of a classic model introduced in 1924.

PARTS OF THE HUNTING RIFLE

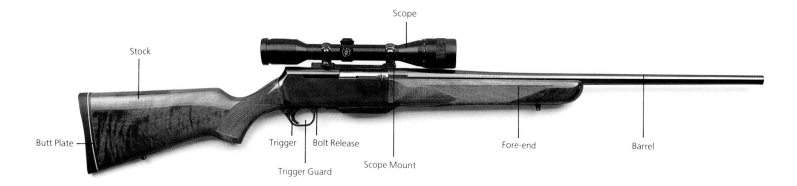

Scope

Stock

Butt Plate

Trigger   Bolt Release

Trigger Guard

Scope Mount

Fore-end

Barrel

RIGHT: To enhance the sport some hunters use scoped .22-caliber rifles for squirrels. This requires an accuracy that comes only through a great deal of practice.

COMPONENTS OF THE CARTRIDGE

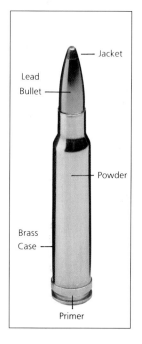

Jacket

Lead Bullet

Powder

Brass Case

Primer

Into the rifle we place the cartridges – note that the bullet is actually only the projectile portion of the overall cartridge. In each caliber these are available in a range of designs and weights (expressed in grains) much too extensive for full discussion here. A few examples will provide some guidance:

For squirrels, a .22 caliber loaded with cartridges that have bullets in the 40- to 45-grain weight range is a good choice. For much white-tail deer hunting, a caliber in the range of .30 to .375, using cartridges with bullets in the 160-200-grain range is optimum. Hunters going after brown bear, on the other hand, would be much more likely to choose something in the .340 to .375 caliber range with a bullet weight of 250 to 300 grains.

Rifles generally come from the factory equipped with one of two basic types of iron sights: the V notch, which offers a rear V with which to align the front bead, and the partridge, which offers a square rear notch.

The type of iron sight that comes as factory-installed equipment has little attraction for many hunters, who immediately equip their rifles with

telescopic scopes, which function much like binoculars, telescopes and telephoto camera lenses. The target is focused in detail on the scope's crosshairs. The advantages in terms of accuracy are obvious.

Scopes are rated in terms of powers, ranging from the least powerful – 1.5x – to the most powerful – 12x. There are also many variable power scopes available, such as 3-9x or 2.5-7x. Scope choice must be dictated by individual circumstances and hunting conditions, but there are a few general considerations. The higher the magnification, the smaller the width of the area that is visible through the scope. And, the higher the magnification the more steadiness required of the hunter to use it successfully.

The other primary design factor of the scope is its reticle, the device inside the tube that marks the exact point for aiming. However, the tried and true crosshairs – formed by the simple crossing of a vertical line with a horizontal line at the center of the viewing area – is probably the most useable for the average hunter.

Handguns

Some hunters also employ handguns – pistols and revolvers – to enhance the challenge in the pursuit of game, but their numbers remain very small. Generally the handgun is a much less accurate weapon than the rifle.

Muzzleloaders, the guns used by the first pioneer hunters of the continent which were eventually replaced by the more efficient and faster breech-loaders, have also been gaining in popularity. They offer a particularly challenging mode of hunting. Many states have enacted special

seasons for muzzleloader hunting, particularly for deer.

There are two basic types of muzzleloaders: flintlock and caplock. Loading the flintlock is a matter of pouring black powder down the bore, followed by a ball with a lubricated patch over it. This is pushed down into contact with the powder

ABOVE LEFT: Scopes of various powers are mandatory for many forms of big game hunting, where the game is generally fired at from great distances.

BOTTOM LEFT: A shot of the Browning 348 Carbine demonstrating its vertical locking system. Dropping the lever drops the lugs from the bolt, allowing the bolt to eject spent cartridges.

by a ramrod. An additional, smaller amount of powder is placed in the gun's pan, where the flint in the hammer will strike. This causes a spark to ignite the powder and fire the rifle. In the case of the caplock, a percussion cap replaces the priming charge of black powder placed in the flintlock's pan.

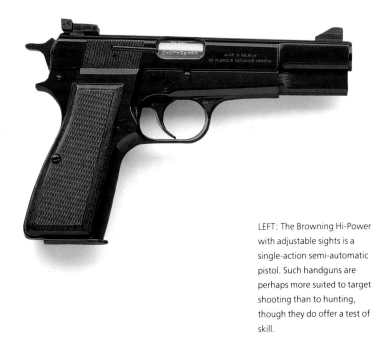

LEFT: Browning's BDA 380 Double Action pistol has a 13-round magazine. It is certainly a compact weapon, weighing only 27 ounces.

LEFT: The Browning Hi-Power with adjustable sights is a single-action semi-automatic pistol. Such handguns are perhaps more suited to target shooting than to hunting, though they do offer a test of skill.

Bows and Arrows

While archery hunting takes another step back towards the primitive in man's pursuit of his quarry, the modern hunting bow is something very different than the bows that the Indians carried. Today's version, known as the compound bow, has a system of pulls and steel pulleys affixed to a bow that's more likely to be made of metal or some space-age material than the wood that formed the earlier prototype. The pulleys allow the archer to draw and hold greater amounts of pressure in the bowstring and to release the string and arrow

RIGHT: A great deal of pre-season practice must precede the actual hunting, whether with bow and arrow or firearm. The hunter owes this kind of preparation to his quarry.

with much greater accuracy. So popular is this type of bow that the traditional recurve – the weapon that the Indians and archery hunters of 20 years ago used – can be difficult to find in some sporting goods stores and catalogs.

Draw weights still vary among bows, generally ranging from 30 or 40 pounds of pull, which is fine for small game, to 60 to 70 pounds, which are required for animals like moose and bear.

Arrows have followed their own evolutionary path from the wooden sticks they were a few decades ago to modern fiberglass, aluminum and carbon. The hunting heads are available in a bewildering array of configurations, each claiming to offer better penetration than the next. A single page in a popular sporting goods' catalog recently featured more than two dozen designs. Personal preference and experience is about the only reliable gauge here.

BELOW: Hunting broadheads are arrow heads for larger game, and are available in a dizzying array of designs. Personal preference combined with the recommendations of knowledgeable archers are the novice's best guide.

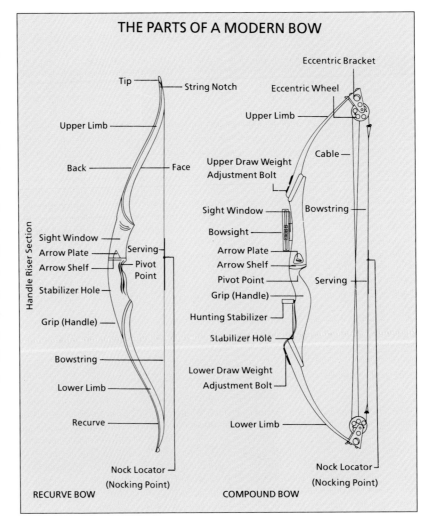

THE PARTS OF A MODERN BOW

RECURVE BOW

Tip — String Notch
Upper Limb
Back — Face
Handle Riser Section
Sight Window
Arrow Plate — Serving
Arrow Shelf — Pivot Point
Stabilizer Hole
Grip (Handle)
Bowstring
Lower Limb
Recurve
Nock Locator (Nocking Point)

COMPOUND BOW

Eccentric Bracket
Eccentric Wheel
Upper Limb
Cable
Upper Draw Weight Adjustment Bolt
Sight Window — Bowstring
Bowsight
Arrow Plate
Arrow Shelf
Pivot Point — Serving
Grip (Handle)
Hunting Stabilizer
Stabilizer Hole
Lower Draw Weight Adjustment Bolt
Lower Limb
Nock Locator (Nocking Point)

ABOVE: The Pearson (Speiler Plus) compound bow offers 55 to 76 pounds of pull.

ABOVE: This compound bow, the Browning Mirage, gives 45 to 70 pounds of pull.

BROADHEADS

Hoyt Chuck-It (100 grains)

Hoyt Blackhole 3 (115 grains)

Thunderhead 125 (125 grains)

Razorback 4 (143 grains)

Satellite Ultimate 3 (120 grains)

Anderson 245 Magnum (125 grains)

Thunderhead 160 (160 grains)

Razorback 5 (143 grains)

Satellite Ultimate 4 (125 grains)

Satellite Magnum 3 (125 grains)

Knives

The hunting knife is an essential piece of equipment that no hunter should go afield without. Mine has served in the traditional tasks of cleaning and skinning game, but it has also tightened a nagging loose screw on a rifle sling and dislodged a jammed rifle cartridge, in addition to countless other now-forgotten tasks.

Personal preference is also the guide in knives, although some – like the outsized Bowie – are much better as display and collector's pieces than as functional field wear. The sheath knife is the standard for most hunters and the optimum blade length for cleaning game is four to six inches. Shorter blades might be a choice for the hunter in pursuit of trophy game heads, as they allow for more detailed skinning out of the head.

Pocketknives find many uses as well, and many hunters drop one of these into their pocket out of habit, even when a perfectly fine sheath knife is already hanging from their belt.

Multibladed knives have little use in a hunting situation. Generally they are bulkier to carry and more cumbersome in use. Finally, after the game has been cleaned, the knife itself will require careful cleaning.

With any knife the top consideration must be how well will it hold a sharp edge. While many manufacturers tout their lines as the best in their category, buying a known long-selling brand is a generally good practice.

LEFT: The choice of a knife is a very personal thing to most hunters. The feel of the blade and the ease of handling are paramount.

Apparel and Special Accessories

Like most other aspects of the sport, hunting apparel and footwear have evolved at an incredible pace over the past few decades. We're now wearing materials like Gore-Tex and Thinsulate which combine twice the warmth and water-resistance with half the weight of anything available to even the previous generation of hunters. Camouflage patterns undreamt of a decade ago are now commonplace, allowing the hunter to blend into anything from the deepest forest through reed-covered marshland to snow-covered fields. In contrast, blaze and fluorescent orange offers the optimum degree of protection from accidental shooting.

TOP RIGHT: A good quality duck or goose call is likely to fool even the wariest bird. These air-operated calls are blown on, like whistles.

BOTTOM RIGHT: Hunting dog accessories are many and varied. Shown here are (top) retrieving and throwing dummies; (center) whistles; and (bottom) collars, bells and leads. All are specially designed in hardwearing materials for field use.

Accessories beyond the basics of weaponry, knives and apparel are too numerous to cover here. Even a book dedicated to such items would be out-of-date before publication. A myriad of dedicated outdoorsman/researchers are providing new insights into product design as well as into the lives of the animals we hunt.

Today the hunter can wash all the scent from himself, his clothing and his equipment. He replaces it with a seductive scent which he trails into his hunting area, permeating it with an odor irresistible to his quarry. Or, he can put out a raft of decoys so lifelike that even he has trouble telling live birds from his fakers. The latest design in calls enables him complete deception with just the right sounds. By means of binoculars, field telescopes and telescopic sights he can spot game at distances so great that no natural sense can come close to matching the range.

Technology has changed the face of hunting and is continuing to change it, but the attractions of the basic sport remain. It will always be a contest between living, breathing creatures: man against his quarry. This is the focus of the next chapters. Throughout most of the book we will discuss the many species that are hunted across the continent. These birds and animals endow the sport with its heart and soul. All the precision instruments and special accessories are merely the means to appreciate that enthralling end.

RIGHT: Deer call kits are available from sporting stores; these include wooden snort, bleat and grunt calls and a tape demonstrating the calling technique for each

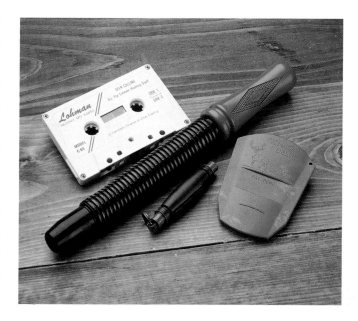

ABOVE: Binoculars enable a hunter to scan great distances for any hint of his game.

BOTTOM RIGHT: Many decoys, such as these for teal, are used less widely in times when hunters voluntarily restrict their hunting for most waterfowl species while populations are down.

Chapter 1

DEER

SUMMER

WINTER

YEAR-ROUND

Whitetail deer

ODOCOILEUS VIRGINIANUS

Of all the animals hunted across North America, no other commands the same attention as the whitetail deer. Whatever measure is used, the whitetail tends to demand the most: the most hunters, most dollars spent on equipment, most hours spent by hunters. An unbelievably adaptable animal, the whitetail has expanded both its range and numbers since the coming of Europeans and their subsequent impact on the natural landscape of the continent, although the resultant increase of the deer has not been steady.

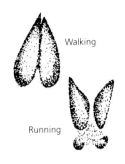

Walking

Running

> *HUNTER'S HINTS*
>
> *When hunting whitetail deer in thick cover, pre-hunt scouting is essential. Find the animals' trails through the area – generally moving between daytime bedding areas and nighttime feeding areas – and then search for signs of the bucks using that area, such as rubs or scrapes.*

RIGHT: The Coues deer (*Odocoileus virginianus covesi*), of the US Southwest, is one of two dwarf subspecies of the whitetail deer. The other is the key deer (*Odocoileus virginianus clavium*), of the Florida Keys.

As the European settlers first changed the land, the whitetail proliferated. Ancient forests of huge trees that had provided little in the way of food or protection for the deer were cleared. Large predators, such as the wolf and mountain lion, were driven from their historical ranges, while the deer that they preyed upon remained. Huge tracts were planted in crops such as corn, grain and fruit. These were as acceptable fodder to the deer as to the men who had planted them.

But, by the dawn of the 20th century, the whitetail deer was on the edge of extinction. Many factors contributed to the drastic decline. Chief among them were the increased hunting of deer for food and hides, including a boom in market-hunting, and the regrowth and maturation of the forests that had been cleared, excluding the deer.

In response to the crisis, whitetails came under full protection for many years in some areas, while only antlered deer were allowed to be taken in

others. In addition, a number of game agencies concentrated great amounts of money and personnel on the whitetail deer that had proved so popular with their license-buying clientele. Habitat and stocking programs were pursued with a vengeance. The protective and restorative efforts worked better than could have been expected. It is generally accepted that there are now more whitetail deer across North America than ever before. This has been accompanied by a notable growth in the number of whitetail deer hunters.

Nearly every hunting method and type of weapon is employed against the animal. Driving, stalking and still-hunting are the three broadly accepted method categories, but each has dozens

ABOVE: Rattling for whitetail deer, with either real deer antlers or synthetic reproductions, has gained much attention among hunters in recent years.

LEFT: A camouflaged archer aims his arrow at a whitetail deer that attempts to sneak by him, apparently aware that something is amiss.

RIGHT: A superb whitetail buck like this wanders the forests of many a hunter's dream. But only those few who put in the time and effort, or those fewer still who experience incredible luck, will actually bag such an animal.

upon dozens of variations devised to deal with specific local conditions. And, given the widespread nature of our modern whitetail population, that includes nearly every local condition below the far north.

ABOVE: A "spooked" whitetail deer can run at slightly over 35 miles per hour for a short distance.

LEFT: A buck rub is just one of the many signs that a whitetail buck leaves in his territory for the trained eye to detect.

Deer Scat

Deer Short Ribs
SERVES 8

4 pounds ribs, cut into 2-inch slices

salt and freshly ground black pepper

1 teaspoon dry mustard

1 tablespoon Worcestershire sauce

½ cup ketchup

½ cup water

¼ cup vinegar

1 medium onion, chopped

1 tablespoon brown sugar

Sprinkle ribs with salt and pepper. Arrange on rack in foil-lined roasting pan. Roast uncovered in a preheated oven at 425°F for 30 minutes. Reduce oven temperature to 350°F. Remove the ribs, discard fat from pan, and return ribs.
Mix together all remaining ingredients and pour over ribs. Cover the pan and bake at 350°F for about 1½ hours, or until tender, turning once halfway through the cooking time.

(RUTH SCHNECK, LATE MOTHER
OF THE AUTHOR)

The average whitetail buck weighs from 125–150 pounds. The average doe is somewhat smaller. And, every year, monsters of 300 pounds or more are taken. Of the couple dozen sub-species – such as the fully protected Keys deer (*Odocoileus virginianus clavium*) in Florida and the Coues deer (*Odocoileus virginianus couesi*) that is hunted in some southwestern states – a few may reach 100 pounds.

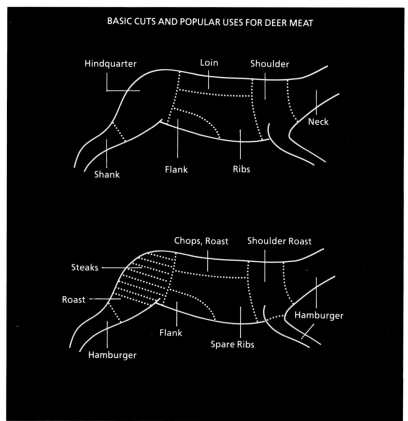

BASIC CUTS AND POPULAR USES FOR DEER MEAT

Hindquarter · Loin · Shoulder · Neck · Shank · Flank · Ribs

Steaks · Chops, Roast · Shoulder Roast · Roast · Flank · Spare Ribs · Hamburger · Hamburger

LEFT: With his trophy downed, a hunter approaches the whitetail buck, alert for any sudden movements on the part of the animal.

All whitetails are gray-brown to red-brown across their entire bodies, except for white on their eponymous tails, and on their bellies, upper throats and chins. Southern whitetails tend to be paler than their northern counterparts. The antlers that define a trophy buck – although some does carry them as well – are shed and regrown each year. Their size is not as age-dependent as is commonly assumed, but much more closely related to food availability and quality.

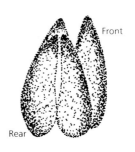

Mule deer

ODOCOILEUS HEMIONUS

A mule deer is a different thing to different hunters in different areas. It might be the sitka, found on several Alaskan islands, about the size of its whitetail cousin. It might be the massive blacktail of the Rockies. Or it might be the sand-tinted muley of America's southwestern desert. All are subspecies.

Using the most general application of the term, the mule deer looks like the whitetail, although with a black-tipped tail. It boasts large mulelike ears and substantially larger and wider antlers.

BELOW: A truly superb mule deer buck will carry a rack of antlers with a spread of as much as 30 inches.

HUNTER'S HINTS

It is always best to hunt moving from the timber towards the open when contouring mountain faces in search of mule deer. Unlike whitetail deer, mule deer rarely sneak through the bush to move behind the hunter. If there is open land ahead the jumped deer is likely to cross it, often offering a good target.

Beer-Baked Venison Chops

SERVES 8

8 chops

seasoned meat tenderizer

pepper

8 teaspoons lemon juice

3–4 tablespoons margarine or oil

8 slices tomato

8 slices green bell pepper

8 thin slices onion

10–11 ounces tomato soup

1 cup beer

¼ teaspoon garlic powder

½ teaspoon basil

¼ teaspoon dry mustard

Remove all fat from the chops. Sprinkle both sides with the tenderizer, pepper, and ½ teaspoon lemon juice. Let the chops sit for 30 minutes.

Heat a skillet and melt the margarine. Sauté the chops until well-browned on both sides. Place the browned chops in a single layer in baking pan. Top each with a slice of tomato, bell pepper and onion.

Combine remaining ingredients in same skillet in which you browned the chops, stirring to pick up any drippings left in the pan. Heat just long enough to thoroughly combine the ingredients. Pour over the chops and bake at 350°F for 1 hour, or until tender.

(FERNE HOLMES, AUTHOR OF *EASY RECIPES FOR WILD GAME AND FISH*, PHOENIX, ARIZ.)

ABOVE: After a successful hunt, two hunters drag their mule deer buck along a snow-covered slope in typical mule deer range.

This traditional mule deer is also a significantly larger animal than the whitetail. Although there is some overlap, mule deer tends to inhabit rougher country than the whitetail. It is found throughout the western portion of the continent, as far east as the Dakotas and Texas.

Many regional populations of mule deer migrate each year to escape the deepest snows that would otherwise hinder their movements and feeding. For some herds, this might mean an almost unnoticeable move down the side of a mountain. For others, the journey might involve almost 100 miles.

In some locales, hunters station themselves along the migration trails that have been worn into the countryside over the years, waiting in ambush. Others might head for the highland plateaux, glassing the slopes in search of the larger bucks that tend to make the move later. Elsewhere the shorelines of scattered islands might be searched for grazing deer by canoe. All of the whitetail hunter's techniques have been applied successfully to the muley.

The mule deer tends to spend most of its waking hours browsing in open, broken areas of low, scattered brush and tall grass, or in the cactus-type habitat of the desert. During inclement

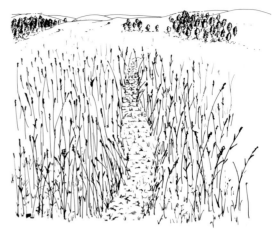

LEFT: General trails are used by many different animal species. They are usually wide and easily spotted. The diversity of animals which use such a trail is usually indicated by such signs as scat or hair.

LEFT: Runs are less obvious than trails, often leading to watering and bedding areas for a single species. Look for signs of recent use; for example, if a run leads to bedding, check for fresh droppings.

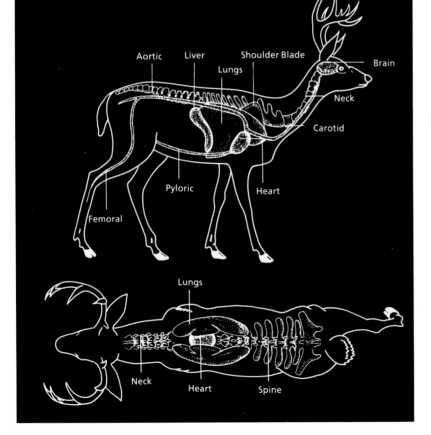

Aortic Liver Shoulder Blade
Lungs Brain
Neck
Carotid
Pyloric Heart
Femoral

Lungs
Neck Heart Spine

LEFT: In a pushdown, vegetation will be bent in the direction of escape. These are not established routes, but may be created by animals being chased by another animal.

weather, heavily wooded areas often shelter the most animals, although the deer tend to avoid these at other times.

Cover is a more crucial factor in locating muleys that it is with whitetails, since the latter are more easily predicted by food availability. The mule deer's diet preferences are extremely wide-ranging. Trees and shrubs are browsed extensively at times, particularly in the winter, while grasses and other herbaceous plants are grazed whenever they can be found.

BELOW: The term "mule deer" is applied to a wide range of subspecies, including this lighter colored desert muley.

Forgotten Steak

SERVES 3–4

2 pounds round deer steak, cut into chunks

1 package dried onion soup mix

2 cups water

Flour and butter for roux

Place ingredients into a skillet. Cover and forget about it for about 1½ hours, or until steak is tender. Thicken the pan juices with a flour and butter roux to make gravy. Serve over rice.

(ELOISE GREEN, NEW MEXICO WILDLIFE, ALAMOGORDIO DAILY NEWS)

Elk

CERVUS CANADENSIS

The American elk, more correctly but less commonly known as the wapiti, ranks among the top big game animals in the world on nearly every hunter's list. An excursion to take on the big deer in its western range is described as a "dream trip" by many an eastern hunter.

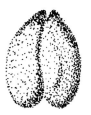

BELOW: A big-beamed bull elk is the object of many a hunter's dream trip "out West." This usually involves the services of a guide and a stay in a mountain base-camp.

When the first Europeans settled along the East Coast of the continent, that as yet undreamt "dream trip" was merely a hike into the woods. The elk's range included nearly all of the United States and southern Canada, even the Plains.

But the massive animal could not adapt to the new presence of humans and retreated into the West's roughest mountain locations before the oncoming westward rush of settlement. The animals were also hunted heavily, as a ready source of meat and because of their competition for grazing areas with domestic livestock. By the early 1900s less than 100,000 remained in isolated pockets.

Game management programs since then have been very successful throughout the elk's western range. A small, totally protected population has even been re-established in Pennsylvania, occasionally growing to the point where limited hunts have been considered.

Much of today's population spends most of the year in mountain meadows above the timberline, or just below it, moving to lower areas for the winter.

Although archers have made inroads into the game, much elk hunting and shooting is done at long range. Guided trips on horseback, operating out of a rugged base camp, are more often than not part of that "dream trip."

In color, the elk is tan in summer, with darker head, mane and limbs, and a buff rump; gray-brown in winter, with similarly darker areas and a thicker mane. Adult bulls weigh from 700 to 1,100 pounds, while the less showy females average from 500 to 700 pounds. Bulls with antlers measuring more than 60 inches in length along the main beams have been taken.

ABOVE: Well-camouflaged, an archer begins calling for elk with a bugle-imitating call.

Braised Elk Steak

SERVES 2–3

1 thick round steak

dripping

freshly ground black pepper

2 cups dry red wine

2 parsnips, cut into small strips

½ to 1 cup turnips, cut into small strips

2 stalks celery, cut into small strips

2 small onions studded with 2 cloves each

Sear the steak in the dripping. Season with pepper and pour over the wine. Add the vegetables, cover and simmer until all is tender and liquid is almost completely evaporated.

(ELOISE GREEN, NEW MEXICO WILDLIFE, ALAMOGORDIO DAILY NEWS)

The largest individuals are members of the subspecies, Roosevelt elk (*Cervus canadensis roosevelti*), which inhabits Pacific coastal forests from northern California into Canada, the Olympic and Cascade mountain ranges, and some Alaskan islands. Conversely, the Roosevelt's antlers tend to be smaller.

Elk have a keen sense of smell and of hearing, but their eyesight is restricted to picking up on moving objects. When spooked, the animal can run at more than 35 miles per hour.

The signature bugling of the bull elk, ending in a long, piercing whistle, can be heard over considerable distances. Decoy calls are popular with hunters during the fall rut to locate bulls. Those males tending harems, as well as those seeking harems, will answer the challenge of what they perceive as another bull's bugle.

LEFT: An elk has good eyesight and hearing; in open country you must be sure to stay quiet and hidden.

Elk Pot Stew

SERVES 6–8

3–5 pounds lean elk, cut into one-inch cubes
flour seasoned with pepper
¼ pound butter or margarine
1 cup chopped onion
1 pound mushrooms, sliced
1 green pepper, pith and seeds removed
1 can bouillon, diluted with water
1 cup red wine
1 can whole corn
4 potatoes
4–6 carrots, sliced thickly

Dredge the elk cubes in the seasoned flour. In a heavy pan melt the butter and sauté the fresh vegetables. Remove the vegetables from the pot and add the meat, searing it on all sides. Add more butter, if necessary. Return the vegetables to the pot and add enough bouillon and water to almost cover the meat and vegetables. Cover and let simmer for almost 2 hours.

Add the wine, corn, potatoes and carrots. Simmer slowly until the vegetables are tender, another 30 minutes or so.

(ELOISE GREEN, NEW MEXICO WILDLIFE, ALAMOGORDIO DAILY NEWS)

Moose

ALCES ALCES

North America has no bigger big game animal than the moose, also the world's largest deer. An adult bull of the largest subspecies, the Alaska moose (*Alces alces gigas*), might weigh in at almost 1,800 pounds and stand nearly eight feet tall. Antler spreads of more than six-and-a-half feet have been taken, but size is more difficult to gauge on a live animal, since the vision of a bull before it takes to the hills can be overpowering in itself.

Despite its great bulk, the moose is surprisingly able to both hide itself efficiently and to move

Running

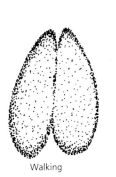

Walking

RIGHT: The moose is the world's largest member of the deer family, sometimes reaching a weight of nearly 1,800 pounds and a height of nearly 8 feet. This bull's antlers are still red with blood during the velvet-shedding period.

Wild Game Meatballs

SERVES 2–3

1 pound ground meat

½ cup fresh bread crumbs

⅓ cup minced onion

¼ cup milk

1 egg

1 tablespoon chopped parsley

1 teaspoon salt

⅛ teaspoon pepper

½ teaspoon Worcestershire sauce

¼ cup oil

10 ounces grape jelly

12 ounces bottled chili sauce

Mix the ground meat, bread crumbs, onion, milk, egg, parsley, salt, pepper and Worcestershire sauce together in a bowl. Shape gently into meatballs. Heat the oil in large skillet and lightly brown the meatballs. Remove meatballs from skillet with a slotted spoon. Stir in the jelly until melted. Add the chili sauce and meatballs, and gently stir until the meatballs are thoroughly coated. Simmer uncovered for 30 minutes. Serve with rice or egg noodles.

(RUTH SCHNECK, LATE MOTHER OF THE AUTHOR)

smoothly through the dense northern forest tangles that it calls home. It is a fixture throughout most of Canada and Alaska, below the Arctic regions. The moose also occurs south along the Rockies as far as New Mexico, in northern New England and in northern North Dakota, Minnesota and Wisconsin. This range is not much diminished in recent times.

Although the moose is the largest deer, hunting techniques are not similar. The big animal is a creature of the wilderness, unable to survive in any numbers close to man's habitations. As a result, moose hunting generally involves the services of a guide.

Hunting techniques vary by region. Western hunting generally involves long-range glassing and shooting in the mountains before the animals move to the lowlands in advance of winter, and similar techniques combined with calling thereafter. The stalk often begins at a distance of several miles.

In the East, moose are generally hunted in much thicker cover and at much closer range. Calling in imitation of the cow during the rut is effective, although it may take hours for an approaching bull to check out the area and decide to reveal himself.

Water is an integral part of the animal's life. Water plants are an important part of the animal's spring through fall diet. In addition, lakes and ponds are the moose's refuge against the black flies, mosquitoes and other insect pests that infest its world during the warmer months.

The moose appears to be almost completely black, even when seen from moderate distances, but its head, back and sides are actually varying shades of very dark brown, while its belly and legs are almost gray. Antlers are quite pale. The body begins in a bulky, hairy chest and tapers into a much thinner rump. The long legs are well adapted to the big deer's penchant for wading to feed on aquatic plants.

RIGHT: A hunter and his guide admire the moose that the latter enabled the former to bag. Guides are essential for successful pursuit of many big game species.

Caribou

RANGIFER SPP

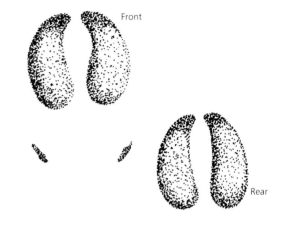

Front

Rear

Some hunters see only a limited challenge in bagging a caribou. The greatest part of the hunt seems to be getting into the animal's range and then selecting a well-antlered male.

In fact, there is some truth to that view. The caribou has never gained the mistrust of man that has become characteristic of other members of the deer family. The caribou may even approach a completely unconcealed hunter out of curiosity.

Furthermore, the caribou is a herd animal and long-developed reliance on sheer numbers is its chief survival mechanism. The caution and

HUNTER'S HINTS

Good optical equipment is crucial when hunting caribou. Although the beasts are not difficult to locate, the standard 7× or 8× binoculars will make them look like tiny specks. On the other hand, a 40× glass is only useful before sunrise or on cool days just before nightfall – the heat haze will distort the image too much. A 20× spotting scope is the ideal tool.

LEFT: The barren ground caribou is the most migratory of the three major types of the species that inhabit the northern reaches of North America.

ABOVE: A hunter maneuvers his canoe back to camp after a successful day of hunting for caribou.

stealth of the solitary animal, such as the whitetail buck, is not part of its northern cousin's nature.

But this relative of the reindeer is just unpredictable enough to make a fallacy out of any of these generalizations whenever a hunter comes to rely upon them as gospel.

The northern reaches of the North American continent, and well south in the east and west, are home to about a dozen subspecies of caribou. They can be grouped into three major types – woodland, barren ground and mountain – but all share the same general characteristics.

Both males and females sport the slightly palmated, rocking-chair antlers with the distinctive forward-protruding shovel-like brow tines. However, those of the male are generally much larger than the female's and larger, relative to body size, than any other deer.

The male of most subspecies stands four feet or less at the shoulder and weighs from 300 to 400 pounds, although some significantly larger individuals have been taken in Alaska. Most are gray-brown to red-brown, with white to yellow on the belly, neck, muzzle, rump and just above the hooves.

Migration is the most widely researched characteristic. The barren ground caribou is the type most given to this food-based activity, and herds of thousands on the move can still be spotted on occasion. At the other extreme is the mountain caribou, that moves to lower, more sheltered areas only during times of severe weather.

Hunting techniques vary among the three major types of caribou. Mountain and woodland caribou are located during the rut on the high ground, where the males are starting to gather their harems of females. After glassing the various bulls that can be seen in the area and selecting one promising rack, the hunter first carefully plans and then slowly makes his stalk, remaining downwind at all times. It is all climaxed, once the hunter is within range, by a carefully planned and executed shot.

Barren ground caribou are generally hunted during the annual move to the winter feeding grounds. Then the hunt is primarily a matter of getting into a good location and picking the trophy head desired.

Sil's Stew
SERVES 8

2 pounds deer, cut into 1-inch cubes

2 tablespoons fat

28 ounces canned tomatoes

4 cups boiling water

1 tablespoon lemon juice

1 tablespoon Worcestershire sauce

1 tablespoon soy sauce

1 clove garlic

1 medium onion, sliced

2 bay leaves

1 tablespoon salt

1 teaspoon sugar

1 beef bouillon cube

½ tablespoon paprika

⅛ teaspoon allspice or cloves

3 large potatoes, diced

1 can peas, drained

6 carrots, sliced

1 can string beans, drained

Thoroughly brown the meat on all sides in the hot fat. Add all other ingredients except the vegetables. Cover, then simmer, but don't boil, for 2 hours, stirring occasionally. Remove the bay leaves. Add the potatoes, peas, carrots and string beans. Cook for 30 minutes more, or until the vegetables are tender. The liquid can be thickened with flour, if desired.

(NORMAN STRUNG, ASSOCIATE EDITOR, *FIELD & STREAM*, FROM HIS BOOK *DEER HUNTING*)

Chapter 2

SQUIRRELS AND MARMOTS

Squirrels

SCIURUS SPP

Each fall millions of squirrels are culled across the continent. Yet game agencies almost universally tell us that the squirrel remains one of our most underharvested game species. The small bushytail ranks with the whitetail deer as one of the most resilient and adaptable of all wildlife on the North American continent.

The name, squirrel, when used by hunters, generally refers to the gray squirrel (*Sciurus carolinensis*), which inhabits the entire eastern half of the continent, and the fox squirrel (*Sciurus niger*), which has expanded its range from Texas through

BELOW : The gray squirrel is generally smaller than the fox squirrel and rarely displays the reddish tints of the latter.

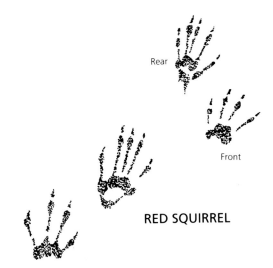

Rear

Front

RED SQUIRREL

the Dakotas east to the Atlantic Ocean. Close relatives are the Arizona gray squirrel (*Sciurus arizonensis*), western gray squirrel (*Sciurus griseus*), and Abert's squirrel (*Sciurus aberti*).

The red squirrel (*Tamiasciurus hudsonicus*) – which occurs throughout the East as far south as the Appalachian Mountains extend, as well as in Alaska, western Canada and some locales in the Rockies – is often found with and near the gray and fox squirrel. However, this smaller squirrel is rarely seen as a game animal and only occasion-ally harvested.

Regardless of the species being pursued, squirrels probably provide the starting point for more hunting careers than any other animals. There are many reasons for this. Once the feeding and nesting area has been located, the bushytails will be available in relatively large numbers. Only under intense hunting pressure will they abandon their normal routine of feeding from first light through late morning, and again from mid-afternoon through last light.

Fried Squirrel

SERVES 6

2–3 squirrels cut into serving-size
pieces
water
juice of ½ lemon
salt and fresh ground black pepper
1 tablespoon garlic powder
½ tablespoon dried parsley
4 tablespoons milk
2 beaten eggs
½ cup flour
½ cup finely ground Ritz crackers
oil

Place the squirrel meat in water to
cover, add the lemon juice, and parboil
for 15–20 minutes. Drain and pat dry
with paper towels. Sprinkle the meat
with a mixture of dry seasonings.
Combine the milk and egg. Dip pieces
in the flour, then in the egg mixture,
then in the cracker crumbs.
Heat ½ inch oil in large skillet. Brown
the squirrel on all sides, then lower
heat and cook until tender, about
20–25 minutes. Drain on paper towels
and serve immediately.

(VICKI SNYDER, FREELANCE OUTDOOR WRITER,
COLUMBUS, OHIO)

LEFT: Squirrels are commonly
spotted in this position which
allows them to somewhat
hide their outline while still
surveying their surroundings.

The adult gray squirrel is about a foot long, with a tail of about the same length, and weighs about a pound. Its coat is a basic gray, with a fine peppering of black and white across its entire body, except for the white belly. Occasionally the white area and some of the face is pale gray or even buff, causing hunters to confuse grays with fox squirrels.

The fox squirrel is a much larger animal, generally one-and-a-half to more than two feet in body length, plus tail, and from one-and-a-half to three pounds in weight. Its coat is primarily gray to reddish-brown-gray, peppered with black, white and shades of brown, and often outlined at the sides in rust. The underside is coloured yellow to orange.

Melanism – black phase – is common in both species, primarily among the fox squirrels in the south and the grays in the north. Albinism is

ABOVE: A large fox squirrel
tumbles from the treetops
after a successful shot.

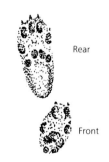

Rear

Front

GREY SQUIRREL

LEFT: Fox versus gray. The fox
squirrel (left) displays much
more reddish and brown
coloring than the gray squirrel
(center). Both species
commonly included
melanistic, or black,
individuals in their population,
like this black gray-squirrel
(right).

TOP: Scared squirrels will often reappear in just a few minutes at the same hole into which they vanished. If they sense that all danger has passed, they will move to the outside of the tree trunk.

ABOVE: Red squirrels are abundant in many areas of North America, but they generally are not considered game animals.

more common in the gray squirrel, and there are some areas that support entire populations of white squirrels.

An area that supports a good squirrel population is easy to identify. The animals' large leaf-cluster nests will be seen in many crooks of both large and small trees. Big, hollow trees will show the signs of the squirrels' comings and goings as worn surfaces at any openings. Cracked nut shells and emptied corn cobs, in woodlands that are close to cornfields, will be abundant.

Both gray and fox squirrels prefer nut-rich woods and are attracted to those wooded areas that lie near to agricultural food sources, particularly corn. It is not uncommon to find both in the same general woodland, but not in the exact same areas of that woodland. The gray squirrel is more inclined to the thicker forest areas, while the fox squirrel tends to be found at the edges.

The most productive means of squirrel hunting is simply to sit on a stump or lean against a tree in an area that shows signs of squirrel activity and wait, scanning both the trees and the ground

Squirrel Pot Pie

SERVES 4–6

2 large squirrels, cut into
6–8 pieces each
water
4 large potatoes, cut into chunks
16 ounces pot pie noodles
1 tablespoon chopped parsley

Place squirrel pieces in water to cover and bring to a boil. Allow to boil for 15 minutes, then turn heat down. Allow to simmer for 1 to 1½ hours, or until meat becomes tender enough to be flaked with a fork. Add potatoes about halfway through the cooking process. After 1 to 1½ hours, add the noodles. Simmer until noodles are tender, adding more water, if necessary. Sprinkle over the parsley before serving, and stir in.

(THE AUTHOR)

for the bushytails. On a still, quiet day, the squirrel's skittering movements through the leaves on the ground often reveals it to the hunter. Its habit of barking at perceived threats can also reveal its location.

Bushytails are also hunted with squirrel dogs, which can be of almost any breed, although those of mixed blood seem to take most readily to the task. The dogs trail the squirrel to the tree it has climbed, then "free it" or hold it there for the hunter who, more often than not, gets the shot on the opposite side.

Marmot

MARMOTA

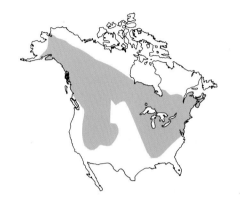

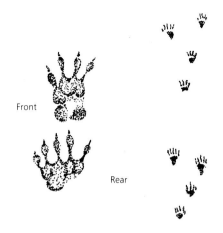

Front

Rear

The woodchuck or groundhog (*Marmota monax*), rockchuck (*Marmota flaviventris*), and hoary marmot (*Marmota caligata*) are distinct species well-adapted to their particular environments. But they are similar enough to be considered as one animal from the hunter's perspective.

All of them spend their lives in relatively small home areas, constantly close to their series of mounded entrance holes, tunnels and dens on an open slope. All are constantly alert to potential dangers in their territories, ready to retreat down the nearest hole at the slightest provocation. These

BELOW : The woodchuck is a widely hunted animal, but too few hunters that pursue the animal actually make use of the meat. (See recipe on page 46.)

are the only true hibernators among the continent's game animals. All three types are hunted by a variety of methods.

Chucks are taken by long-distance gunners with heavily powered and scoped rifles rested on mounds of sandbags, by stalkers with iron sight .22s, and by archers crouching in tall weeds to wait for the whistle-pig to emerge from its nearby burrow. In most areas the chucks remain classified as varmints rather than as game animals, because of the agricultural community's sentiments against them and the damage they can do to fields and crops. For this reason there generally exists no closed season on the animals.

The woodchuck is smaller than its two cousins,

weighing as much as a dozen pounds and measuring two feet or more as an adult. It is mottled brown to red-brown throughout its body, with a small, darker, bushy tail. A pair of long incisors protrudes down from its upper lip.

The rockchuck can be more than two feet long and weigh as much as 16 pounds. A yellow-brown coat covers most of its body, except for yellow on the belly and feet, and white around the mouth.

With the exception of the porcupine and beaver, the hoary marmot is the largest of all North American rodents. It can weigh as much as 20 pounds and measure nearly three feet, from head to tail. The coat is grayish with black flecking, except for black at the feet and tail.

ABOVE: Much woodchuck hunting is done at long range with a scoped rifle.

Woodchuck Pie
SERVES 2–3

1 young woodchuck, cut into
2–3 pieces
water
¼ cup chopped onion
¼ cup chopped green pepper
½ tablespoon minced parsley
salt
⅛ teaspoon pepper
1 cup plus 2½ tablespoons flour
2 teaspoons baking powder
2 tablespoons fat
¼ cup milk

Parboil the woodchuck pieces for 1 hour. Remove the meat from the bones in large chunks. Add the onion, pepper, parsley, 1 tablespoon salt, the pepper, and 2½ tablespoons flour to the broth from parboiling.
Measure out the mixture into a baking dish; if there is less than 3 cups, add more water. Return the meat to the broth in the dish and stir.
Sift 1 cup of flour, baking powder and salt together in a bowl. Cut in the fat, add the milk and stir until the dry ingredients are moist. Work into a dough, then roll out. Cover the meat in baking dish with the dough. Place in a preheated 400°F oven and bake for 40 minutes, or until the dough is golden and puffed.

(PENN. STATE COOPERATIVE EXTENSION SERVICE)

WHITE-TAILED

BLACK-TAILED

Prairie dog

CYNOMYS SPP

Prairie dog towns covering a couple hundred miles and housing hundreds of millions of the small ground squirrels were commonly recorded by the pioneers crossing the American plains. Those early reports may be more or less accurate, but it can be taken as fact that the coming of the settlers, their clearing of the land and their destruction of the rodents' natural enemies, led to a population boom among the prairie dogs.

RIGHT: Although prairie dog populations have plummeted drastically since the European settling of the West, some sizeable towns can still be found.

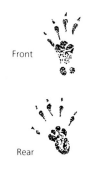

Front

Rear

So successful was the small animal in this altered environment that, by 1900, the prairie dog was seen as one of the most destructive of agricultural pests. Large scale, government-supported poisoning efforts were launched across North America. Today the prairie dog is gone from much of its historic range and there are no hundred-mile area/million-occupant towns to be found anywhere. Nevertheless some towns do still exist and prairie dogs do provide exciting sport in some areas of America.

From a hunter's perspective, the prairie dog can be viewed as a woodchuck in miniature. Much of the hunting, however, is done at long-range with scoped rifles. In addition the prairie dog tends to be much more communal than the woodchuck, generally relying on one sentry for the safety of the group.

There are several species of prairie dog in the American West, most notably the black-tailed (*Cynomys ludovicianus*) and the white-tailed (*Cynomys leucurus*). They are all rather similar, with short heavy bodies, broad heads and short hairy tails. The coat varies from reddish-brown to buff, with a much paler belly.

Several species of ground squirrel (*Spermophilus spp*) are also hunted within their ranges, mostly in the west and north. In general, within the local circumstances, they are hunted much like the chucks and prairie dogs.

BELOW: Many species of ground squirrel are hunted, although much more for target practice than for the animal's meat. This is a Columbian ground squirrel.

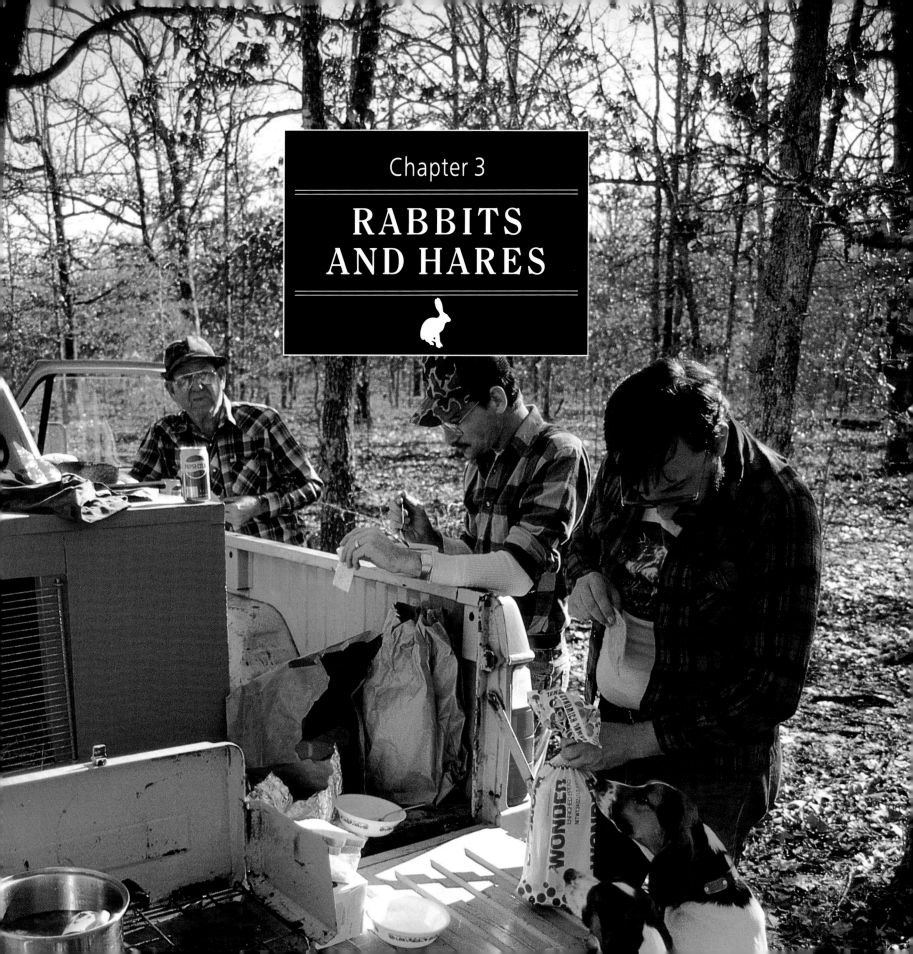

Chapter 3

RABBITS AND HARES

Cottontail rabbit

SYLVILAGUS SPP

Nearly every hunter across the US – except in the far West, and well into southern Canada – is familiar with the small blur of fur known as the cottontail rabbit. For most, the name is applied to the eastern cottontail (*Sylvilagus floridanus*), which inhabits every area of the eastern part of the continent except northern New England. However, there are several other primary types, including the New England (*Sylvilagus transitionalis*), which ranges from southeastern Canada to Alabama; swamp (*Sylvilagus aquaticus*), which is found in the southern and southcentral states; marsh (*Sylvilagus palustris*), which inhabits a limited range from Virginia south; Rocky Mountain (*Sylvilagus nuttalli*), which ranges from the plain states to the Sierra Nevadas; and Audubon

BELOW: A well-hidden cottontail rabbit remains motionless but ready to spring into a dead run as a hunter approaches its hiding place (at the base of the tree).

(Sylvilagus auduboni), which is found from Oklahoma to the Southwest and the Rockies.

Wherever it's found – and that is usually in or very near thick brushy areas – the cottontail rabbit is a top game animal. Able to sit motionless in some secluded patch of weeds for unbelievable lengths of time, the bunny can then, at the last minute, burst away at 20 miles per hour in a zigzagging fashion.

It can lead a pack of beagles in a mile-long circle, only to return to sanctuary nearly back at the starting point. Only when the dogs press it extremely hard will the rabbit "hole up."

Cottontails in general are gray-brown across the body, often with a peppering of black and white along its back. The belly and small cotton-like tail are usually white with some bluish under-fur. The animals weigh from two to three-and-a-half pounds and measure up to two feet in length.

Bunnies are well-suited to a lifestyle based on hiding. A hunter can walk within a few feet of one that has concealed itself in a thick patch of tangles and never see the animal. Some experienced hunters are able to spot these hidden rabbits by their black eyes. A few even hunt the animals at a distance with a scoped, small-caliber rifle, picking them out by means of their tell-tale eyes.

In areas of heavy hunting pressure, the cotton-tail sometimes adapts to a largely nocturnal life-style. On mornings after a fresh snowfall a surprising number of tracks can often be found in areas presumed to have only limited rabbit populations. In these areas, rainy fall days often find the bunnies out and about during the daylight hours. Under all conditions, the best time of day for rabbit hunting is early morning and late afternoon.

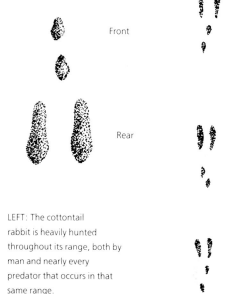

Front

Rear

LEFT: The cottontail rabbit is heavily hunted throughout its range, both by man and nearly every predator that occurs in that same range.

ABOVE: Beagles bay as they cross a path, hot on the trail of an Arkansas cottontail rabbit.

Snowshoe rabbit

LEPUS AMERICANUS

Also known as the varying hare, snowshoe rabbits are common from Alaska and northern Canada, south along the Rockies and Appalachians well into the US, although they become less common farther south.

A creature of the wilderness, the snowshoe does not fare well in the face of man's developments. However, as forests in parts of northeastern states have been allowed to grow back after logging, some

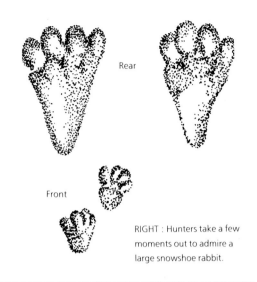

Rear

Front

RIGHT : Hunters take a few moments out to admire a large snowshoe rabbit.

ABOVE: The name of varying hare seems more appropriate than snowshoe rabbit when the animal is in the process of changing from its winter white to summer brown or vice versa.

RIGHT: The snowshoe rabbit is a tough, challenging quarry that can lead a pack of beagles on a lengthy chase across a snow-covered landscape.

reintroduction efforts have proven successful.

In summer, varying hare seems a much more appropriate name. The animal is red-brown to gray-brown across most of its body, with a white belly and underside of the tail.

With fall, the snowshoe name becomes the more obvious choice, as the hare's coat begins the transformation to almost pure white throughout, except for the tips of the three- to four-inch ears. The name is also apt in view of the animal's huge, heavily furred hind feet.

The snowshoe rabbit measures about one-and-a-half to two feet in length and weighs as much as five pounds. The Arctic hare, with which the snowshoe is sometimes confused, can be two-and-a-half feet long and as heavy as 12 pounds.

Good snowshoe hunting is a cyclic thing, as is the snowshoe population. Under natural conditions, the population tends to boom every nine to 12 years.

Dogs are a key element in effective snowshoe hunting. Beagles, foxhounds and crosses of the two are the common choice. The hare displays the same circling technique when being pursued as the cottontail rabbit, but its larger size and snowshoed feet allow it to take the dogs on a much longer chase. Several decreasing circles may be followed by a prolonged pursuit though, alternatively, the chase might be much shorter, with the hare quickly giving the dogs the slip.

Some hunters are able to take snowshoes without dogs. This requires sneaking slowly and quietly through likely areas, watching for the eyes and ear-tips or the slight movement that the hare often makes before exploding from its hiding place in a cloud of snow.

Jackrabbit

LEPUS SPP

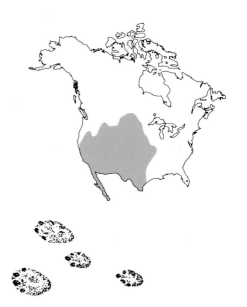

Close relatives of the snowshoe hare, jackrabbits are found throughout the western half of the continent. The black-tailed (*Lepus californicus*) is the most common and widespread, and has been introduced with some success as far east as New Jersey. The white-tailed (*Lepus townsendi*) inhabits only a slightly smaller range and is generally considered to be both more challenging and better table fare. The antelope jackrabbit (*Lepus alleni*) occupies a much more limited range, from New Mexico south.

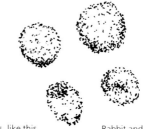

BELOW: Jackrabbits, like this black-tailed jackrabbit, can readily outrun nearly every breed of dog and so hunters generally do not employ dogs in their pursuit of this quarry.

Rabbit and Hare Scat

Baked Rabbit

SERVES 2–3

1 whole rabbit, hare or squirrel

garlic powder

onion powder

1 large carrot, cut into rings

1 stalk celery, cut into chunks

1 large onion, cut into chunks

1 large potato, cut into chunks

margarine

Rub entire rabbit, inside and out, with garlic and onion powders. Place on a broad sheet of aluminum foil. Stuff the cavity with the vegetables and several pats of margarine, and lay several pats of margarine along the carcass of the rabbit. Bring the foil up around the sides of the rabbit and seal at the top. Place in a preheated 325°F oven and cook for about 1¼ hours, until the meat becomes tender.

Open the foil and fold down to expose the rabbit; cook for another 15 minutes, or until the meat is golden brown and tender.

(THE AUTHOR)

All three species tend to be most active during the very early morning and late afternoon. During most of the day they are commonly jumped in their resting spots – called forms – which they scrape out of the earth under thick brush.

Dogs are used much less in jackrabbit hunting than in the pursuit of other North American hares and rabbits. The large, lanky rabbits are able to outpace nearly every breed of dog and they rarely circle when pursued, choosing a straight escape route instead.

In areas of light cover hunters often use small-caliber rifles equipped with scopes to take jackrabbits that can be spotted at some distance. If the cover is thick, a hunter can sometimes stalk to within shotgun range of the hares, who tend to try to sit in concealment when first threatened. When the jack does erupt at the last possible moment, it will often stop and look back after bounding only a few dozen yards.

The black-tailed jackrabbit is about two to two-and-a-half feet long and weighs as much as eight pounds. Its coat is light gray-brown, with off-white on the belly, and black at the ear-tips, top of tail and rump.

The white-tailed is slightly smaller, at less than two feet in length and under 10 pounds in weight. Some populations, mostly in the northern extent of the range, change to a winter white or pale gray, like the snowshoe rabbit. Otherwise, its coat is tan to gray with black ear-tips, white belly and white tail.

The antelope jackrabbit is the smallest – about a foot-and-a-half long and seven pounds at most – but its non-tipped ears may be a full eight inches long. Its coat is pale brown, fading into off-white on its side and belly.

Chapter 4

UPLAND BIRDS

Ruffed Grouse

BONASA UMBELLUS

Across its widespread range the ruffed grouse is also known as the partridge, wood partridge, willow grouse, pine hen and mountain pheasant.

The average male weighs one-and-a-quarter to one-and-a-half pounds, and measures 15 to 20 inches in length, including a five- to seven-and-a-half-inch tail that ends in a semi-rounded arch. In general, a tail that can be fanned into a full half-circle belongs to a male bird. Wingspan is about two feet. The average female is one-quarter to one-sixth less in weight and length.

BELOW: During the springtime mating season the male ruffed grouse 'drums' on a specially selected drumming log within its range to proclaim its territory and attract a mate. The drumming sound is produced through the rapid beating of the bird's wings.

Most hunters know the ruffed groused as little more than a thundering blur of feathers exploding from a dense thicket, often behind them. Although the grouse has been clocked at slightly more than 50 miles per hour in flight, it tends to move at about 25 miles per hour in thickly wooded areas. The bird can fly a quarter mile or more when crossing a large open area, such as a field, but the average flight covers much less ground, as the grouse usually settles in the first substantial bit of cover.

An alert hunter can sometimes "mark" the spot where a missed bird has landed and flush him a second, sometimes even a third, time. Often the bird will hold tighter on subsequent points or approaches.

The ruffed grouse is a mottled array of browns and gray across its head, back and sides, and buff to gray on its underside. Irregular darker and lighter bands, bars, spots and eyespots are scattered throughout. Both sexes have the head crest and neck ruff, although both are more evident on the male. Over each eye the grouse has a flap of skin that tends to be pinkish on the male and grayish on the female.

The bird's legs are covered with feathers almost to the toes, which are fringed with flat cuticle sections known as pectinations. Both of

BELOW: Hunters and their dogs push through typical blue grouse habitat in Colorado.

ABOVE: The blue grouse is a species similar to the eastern ruffed grouse but with a much more limited range. It is found primarily in the Rocky and Sierra Nevada mountains and along the northern Pacific coast.

these physical characteristics are adaptations to the snow and cold that comes to nearly all of the ruffed grouse's range each winter.

No other non-migratory game bird comes close to the range of the ruffed grouse, which is found from mid-Canada south into Georgia and Tennessee in the East, from Alaska south into northern California in the West. About a dozen different subspecies have been identified, ranging from the brownish eastern ruffed grouse to the most widespread gray ruffed grouse of Canada and the US Rockies.

Much of the ruffed grouse's range correlates directly to the distribution of aspen, the buds of which are the most important food for the bird. However, tangles of wild grapes, blueberry patches, stands of sumac, rhododendron thickets and high-yield nut-tree forests are generally productive spots in the East, as are clover patches near wooded areas in the Midwest.

There are about a dozen subspecies of the ruffed grouse, occuring in various portions of the bird's range. In addition, the spruce grouse (*Canachites canadensis*) and the blue grouse (*Dendragrapus obscurus*) are also related closely enough in habit and habitat preference to be discussed here.

The spruce grouse is only about 16 inches long. Males are gray with black markings above, a darker underside with white patches, a black throat and a small red comb. Females are brown-gray with small patches of black, tan and olive above, and off-white with brownish patches on the underside.

The blue grouse is large, often larger than the ruffed grouse, measuring about 22 inches in length. Males are gray, mottled with brown and black above, and white below, with a yellowish comb and small yellowish air sacs at the sides of his neck. Females are brown, mottled in darker brown, without the comb or air sacs.

BELOW: The ruffed grouse is a worthy adversary for any shotgunner. It is an explosive flusher and swift flyer, whose exact actions can rarely be anticipated.

Sage grouse

CENTROCERCUS UROPHASIANUS

The sage grouse is known by many names throughout its range: hen, chicken, turkey, buzzard – all with the word sage in front of them. Each fall these birds migrate short distances to the south within their ranges, gathering in small, loosely knit flocks.

Although the replacement of historical sage ranges with grazing lands for cattle has hurt the overall sage grouse population, it is still found from the Pacific Coast states east through the Plains states.

The sage grouse is America's largest grouse and is second only to the wild turkey among the continent's gallinaceous birds. Males can weigh as much as eight pounds and range up to two-and-three-quarter feet in length. Hens weigh four pounds on average and are as long as two feet. Both are gray-brown, mottled darker, above, and black on their undersides. The male sports a white chevron across its throat, a black chin and a yellow comb.

Gathering at breeding leks early each spring, each male claims and defends a small territory, where he displays for the females. Subsequent hatching occurs in May and June, with the chicks joining the flocks where they will be found through the fall and winter.

As the name implies, sage is a chief food source, but clover and alfalfa will also be heavily consumed. Field edges, ditches, sloughs and sage flats are all productive areas for the hunter of sage grouse. The birds tend to congregate at water during the day, leaving ample evidence of their presence in the form of tracks in the mud and mottled droppings.

Unlike many upland gamebirds, the sage grouse flock tends to flush only a few birds at a time, offering the hunter several shooting opportunities over a short distance. The flush is also generally slower than that of many other gamebirds, making this a good "training prey" for new hunters.

Sage Grouse Breast in Crockpot

SERVES 3–4

1 large breast, skinned
4 stalks celery, sliced
4 large carrots, scraped and sliced
8 ounces tomato sauce
1 cup water
1 tablespoon dried vegetable flakes
¾ cup uncooked elbow macaroni
salt and freshly ground black pepper

Place the sliced celery and carrots in bottom of a crockpot. Place sage grouse breast on top of vegetables. Add the tomato sauce, water and vegetable flakes. Cover and cook on high heat for 6–7 hours, or until the meat is fork-tender.
Remove the breast from the crockpot and when cooled, cut into bite-sized pieces. Return the meat pieces to the pot and add macaroni. Cover and cook on high heat until macaroni is done and liquid is absorbed. Season with salt

(JOAN CONE, FREELANCE OUTDOOR WRITER, WILLIAMSBURG, VA.)

Grape- and Nut-Stuffed Grouse

SERVES 2

1 large grouse
¾ cup butter or margarine
½ teaspoon thyme
30 seedless grapes
1 cup chopped nut meats

Melt the butter and add thyme and pepper to it. Mash half the grapes and add them to the mixture. Rub the bird thoroughly, inside and out, with this mixture. Place bird on large piece of aluminum foil, bringing foil up at the sides. Stuff the remaining grapes and all of nut meats into the body cavity. Pour some of the butter mixture made earlier into the cavity and dribble rest of it over the body of the bird. Seal foil around the grouse. Place the bird in a preheated 350°F oven for 35 minutes, or until the meat begins to become tender to a fork. Open the foil to expose the bird and cook for another 10 minutes, basting at least once, until the meat browns slightly.

LEFT : A male sage grouse in full display struts for a couple of females on his breeding lek.

Sharp-tailed grouse

PEDIOECETES PHASIANELLUS

The sharp-tailed grouse averages 16 to 19 inches in length. Both sexes are brown to yellow-brown, with darker patches above, white patches on the wings, and an off-white underside with brown chevrons. Males have a yellow to reddish comb and orangish air sacs on the sides of their necks.

The bird ranges from Alaska east to Quebec and south to the Northwest and the Great Lakes region. Grain fields hold a particular attraction for the sharp-tailed grouse, and a water source close at hand is a clincher. Nearby thick vege-tation is also productive, as are thickets and stands of trees such as willow, birch, alder and ash.

Males establish their small territories on the congregational breeding leks each fall, returning to use them in courtship and mating in the spring.

Sharp-tailed grouse may roost high in the branches of thickly-growing trees, and often are out of range before the ground-attuned hunter fully realizes he has flushed them.

The bird is also known as the white-bellied and pintail grouse.

BELOW: The male sharp-tailed grouse sets up his preferred breeding leks in the fall and then returns there in the spring for mating.

Pinnated grouse

TYMPANUCHUS CUPIDO

BELOW: When many male prairie chickens gather together during the spring mating season, their booming (which the birds produce by forcing air from sacs on their necks) can be heard for more than a mile.

More commonly known as the prairie chicken, only two subspecies are hunted: the lesser, which ranges from New Mexico east through Kansas, and the greater, which ranges from Kansas and Oklahoma north through South Dakota.

Prairie chickens tend to follow regular, morning flight paths between feeding and roosting spots, and hunters can take advantage of pass shooting similar to that of waterfowl. The birds can fly at about 40 miles per hour. Foods favored by this species are sorghum, wheat, corn and oats, but weed plants also form part of their diet.

Both sexes are tan to yellowish brown, paler below, with darker bars across their bodies. Patterned white spots and bars are found across the wings. Dark quills (also called pinnae) are found on the sides of the neck, extending above the male's head. The male also has an orange comb that the female lacks.

The booming, three-noted call of the males can be heard at more than a mile distance from their breeding leks.

Chukar partridge

ALECTORIS CHUKAR

The chukar partridge is a European immigrant to North America, introduced into nearly all states and provinces on the continent during the 20th century but with limited success. Such efforts have fared better since an understanding of the bird's need for dry, rocky habitat has come about. Today's population ranges from the northwestern US and southwestern Canada east into the Plains states.

Grassy vegetation, such as fiddleneck ferns or bunchgrass, are the primary food of the chukar partridge, but man's grain fields are also visited regularly when nearby. Roosting, hiding and nesting is accomplished in thick brush. Steep slopes and water sources must be located nearby.

Coveys range from six to 50, with an average of about two dozen birds. Early morning will find the group on warmer slopes; mid-morning in preferred feeding areas; midday through late afternoon near water.

The birds tend to run uphill as their first-choice route of escape and, when cut-off, flush downhill. A flushed and scattered flock can be located as

singles, pairs and small groups through their regrouping "chuk-ar" calls. These smaller groupings tend to hold tighter.

The chukar partridge is also known locally as the rock partridge, red-legged partridge and gray partridge.

ABOVE: Chukars prosper in areas that most species would consider less inviting, but do poorly in rich farmland regions.

FACING PAGE: The chukar produces the call from which its name arises as a means of keeping the covey together or regrouping when the birds do become scattered.

Hungarian partridge

PERDIX PERDIX

Like the chukar partridge, the Hungarian partridge is an immigrant from Europe. Its American name derives from the fact that most of the early introductions were of Hungarian stock. Those early efforts, in Washington and California, had limited success.

Subsequent stockings, in areas more closely resembling the bird's native prairies, were much more successful. Today's population is scattered from the West Coast states and Canadian provinces east to Ohio and Ontario. Scattered populations can be found even into the New England states.

Although the Hungarian partridge can thrive in wildlands, local populations are invariably drawn into any nearby agricultural fields. In farming regions, a high proportion of the bird's fall diet consist of agricultural crops.

This partridge generally flocks in small coveys that flush at considerable distances. But the birds tend to return to the spot of the original flush after a subsequent flush or two. Late season coveys are often larger than those of the first days of hunting, as a few females and their offspring of the year band together.

Ring-necked pheasant

PHASIANUS COLCHICUS

Even the most publicity-minded game agencies across the country today must admit that there is something terribly wrong with our populations of the highly popular ring-necked pheasant.

Habitat loss seems to be the primary reason for the bird's incredible decline. Nearly ever hunter with more than a decade's worth of experience can point to more than a few former favored fields

Fruited Pheasant

SERVES 2

2 pheasant breasts, skinned and boned

juice of 1 lemon

3 tablespoons butter

chopped parsley

8 apricot or peach halves

Sauce

½ cup yogurt

½ cup mayonnaise

1 teaspoon curry powder

1 tablespoon butter (optional)

Divide the lemon juice and butter between the pheasant breasts, sprinkle with parsley, and place four fruit halves on each. Roll them up, hold tight and wrap in tin foil. Bake for 35 minutes in a preheated 375°F oven.

Combine the yogurt, mayonnaise and curry powder and allow to come to room temperature or warm with the butter, if desired.

Slice pheasant and pour the room temperature or warmed sauce over it.

(RUTH SCHNECK, LATE MOTHER
OF THE AUTHOR)

and wetlands that are today housing developments and shopping centers. In those remaining fields, edge-to-edge agriculture has eliminated any semblance of the bramble thickets that once afforded protection.

The continuing loss of this magnificent game-bird is a real tragedy, because fewer members of future generations will come to know the cackling explosion of feathers that is the flushed cock-bird. The bird levels at around 25 feet, moving at about 35 miles per hour in alternating wing-beating and gliding.

The male averages about three feet in length, but nearly half of that is made up of the long, bown and black-barred tail feathers. The bird actually weighs only two to three pounds. Its head is black with a coating of irridescent green and violet. The featherless, bright red comb and wattle come together around the eyes. The species'

primary common name is derived from the bright white ring around the male's neck, although this feature is not always present. The body feathers range throughout nearly all shades of brown.

The female is somewhat smaller and much more drab than the male. Her body color is subdued, in pale shades of brown, mottled with some black and white.

The ring-necked pheasant was one of the earliest game animals imported into North America. George Washington enjoyed his days wingshooting the birds he had brought to his lands, although such early efforts met with only limited success.

During the mid-1900s, the ring-necked pheasant had reached its highest numbers across much of the United States and the southern few hundred miles of Canada, and limits seemed to be the expected norm. Changing agricultural methods have since changed that situation, and much hunting today is sustained only with game-farm reared birds that are generally ill-equipped

Schwartz Valley Pheasant Breasts

SERVES 2

2 large pheasant breasts, filleted and skinned

dash of sage

grated Parmesan cheese

slices of Swiss and Cheddar cheese

bacon slices

butter

marjoram

thyme

¼ cup diced onion

crushed garlic

¾ cup sliced raw mushrooms

½–¾ cup good white wine

½ cup heavy cream

On a flat surface, loosely wrap the breast fillets in waxed paper and pound thin with a wooden mallet. Dust each breast with sage and the grated Parmesan cheese, top with several slices of Swiss and Cheddar, and one bacon strip. Roll tightly and close with toothpick, snipping off any cheese or bacon that protrudes from meat. Melt the butter in skillet, brown the meat, remove, then add the onion, garlic and the remaining spices. Stir in the mushrooms and sauté until brown. Pour over the wine, bring to simmer, and return the meat to the skillet. Cover lightly, cook on a bubbling simmer for 15–20 minutes (more for older bird), turning meat occasionally with tongs to avoid puncturing. Adding more wine, if needed. Remove the meat to a heated platter.

Raise heat and reduce liquid. Stir in the cream and warm sauce through, but avoid boiling. Serve immediately with mushroom sauce over meat.

(SCOTT WEIDENSAUL, FREELANCE OUTDOOR WRITER, SCHYULKILL HAVEN RD, PA.)

to survive in the wild. A very large percentage of the ring-necked pheasant's diet consists of seeds and grains.

Everything from brush lines at the edge of cultivated fields, through stubble fields and dense tangles of small trees and brush, to large wooded swamps are prime hunting grounds for this spirited bird. Individuals and small groups tend to spend the early morning and late afternoon hours further outside of cover than during the rest of the day, more so during the early days of the hunting season.

RIGHT: With a resounding cackle a male ring-necked pheasant, generally referred to as a cockbird, bursts from its hiding place.

Sichuan pheasant

PHASIANUS COLCHICUS STRAUCHI

In response to the decline of the ring-necked pheasant population, a few states have started efforts to introduce a new species onto the American landscape – the Sichuan pheasant. Touted as a bird that leads a lifestyle close to that of the ruffed grouse, it is expected therefore to be able to survive in the face of declining ring-neck habitat.

Michigan imported the first birds from China before that country closed all exportation of pheasant and many other creatures. Pennsylvania obtained a few cockbirds from Michigan and began breeding them with ring-neck hens.

Although birds in both programs – pure Sichuans in Michigan and crossbred Sichuan-ring-neck in Pennsylvania – have demonstrated some success when released into the wild, both efforts are still in their infancy.

* EXPERIMENTAL, SMALL POPULATIONS

ABOVE: Hunting preserves, such as Martz's Gap View Hunting Preserve in central Pennsylvania, offer pheasant hunting the way it used to be and with many added amenities such as well-trained dogs and handlers.

RIGHT: A pheasant remains frozen in its brushy hiding place as an approaching dog follows the scent of the bird.

Mourning dove

ZENAIDURA MACROURA

The mourning dove has earned a reputation for causing hunters to spend an inordinately high number of shells for every bird bagged. It is a record unrivaled by most other gamebirds. Four, five or six shots for every hit is not exceptional.

Capable of flight speeds of up to 60 miles per hour in short bursts, it averages 40 miles per hour over longer distances. The bird can also turn sharply "on a dime" and be out of range in an instant. The body is deceptively small, only about half of its 12- to 14-inch length, and as a result many shots are placed well behind any kill zone.

The mourning dove is gray-brown, though some having almost a pinkish cast over their feathers. The wings are darker, and a black cheek spot is found on each side of the face. Sexes are similar in color, but females are paler and generally smaller.

Early season doves are mostly local birds that follow established flight paths, from food to water to roost, at nearly the same time each day, until they become skittish under heavy hunting pressure. These patterned flights generally take place

LEFT: Mourning doves show a decided preference for landing in trees near feeding and watering areas. Decoys can be placed in such trees to encourage the small birds into shotgun range.

ABOVE: A freshly harvested cornfield acts as a magnet on all doves within the area.

from early- to mid-morning and again in the late afternoon. Throughout much of the season the remaining locals that do not begin their southerly migration will be joined by incoming migrants.

Nearly every type of grain field will draw mourning doves in good numbers, but millet fields are probably the most favored, followed by cornfields that have been cleared by automatic harvesting equipment. The bird also thrives on a diet of weeds, when agricultural crops are not available.

Doves Marie

SERVES 4–6

12–16 doves, whole birds or breasts,
cleaned and plucked

¼ cup chopped onion

½ cup chopped celery

1 cup quartered mushrooms

2 tablespoons butter

½ teaspoon oregano

¼ teaspoon basil

salt and pepper to taste

1 tablespoon soy sauce

1½ cups light cream

parsley sprigs

Arrange doves in a buttered, shallow baking dish. In a frying pan, gently sauté the onion, celery and mushrooms in the butter for 5 minutes. Add the seasonings, soy sauce and cream. Bring to the boiling point. Pour the sauce over the doves, cover the baking dish and bake in a preheated 350°F oven for 1 hour.

Twice during the cooking, remove the dish from the oven and turn the birds in the sauce. Cook some wild rice in plenty of salted water for 40 minutes.

Drain thoroughly and add butter. Arrange on serving platter. Place the doves around the rice and spoon the sauce over both. Garnish with parsley.

(SYLVIA BASHLINE, FREELANCE OUTDOOR WRITER, SPRUCE CREEK, PA, FROM HER BOOK *BOUNTY OF THE EARTH COOKBOOK*)

Tree lines or high weeds near feeding areas and waterholes are excellent ambush spots because the birds often land in trees to survey the situation before landing to feed or drink. They slow their flight before landing. Similar ambush situations are also possible where the birds roost for the night, at least during the early weeks of the season.

Camouflage is generally necessary for such ambushing. Decoys are also available, but they will serve only to bring the birds marginally closer and will not cause the birds to glide in for a landing.

Early in the season, walking slowly through weed fields or harvested agricultural fields in a zigzagging pattern will flush a good number of birds, often in twos and threes. Later in the season they will tend to flush too far out to make this method worthwhile.

Over much of its range the mourning dove is referred to simply as the dove. In some locales, it is also known as the turtle dove or Carolina dove.

The white-winged dove (*Zenaida asatica*) is closely related to the mourning dove, although it is much more restricted to a southwestern US range. The local populations tend to fluctuate wildly from year to year.

In appearance, the white-winged is similar to the mourning dove, except for being somewhat stockier and having large white patches on its wings and at the rear corners of its tail. It does not present as twisting and turning a target as the mourning dove, but it is nonetheless a challenging gamebird. It too requires the hunter to go afield with an ample supply of shells. Like the mourning dove, early season birds are much less wary than those that remain later in the season.

White-winged doves follow many of the same daily patterns and habits as their mourning cousins and can be taken with the same techniques. However, the bird is more migratory overall and the best late-season shooting occurs south of the Rio Grande River, where large numbers gather for the winter.

Other common names are whitewing, singing dove and Sonora dove.

RIGHT: Ambush hunting along the regular daily flight paths of the dove is generally the most successful method of hunting the birds.

Willow ptarmigan

LAGOPUS LAGOPUS

The willow ptarmigan occurs worldwide in one subspecies or another. About a half-dozen of these are found on the North American continent.

Males are about 16 inches long and weigh about one-and-a-half pounds. Their primary and secondary feathers are white year-round while most of the white-tipped tail remains brown. The rest of their other feathers alternate between white in the winter and brown in the summer. Males sport a bright red comb which females lack.

Of the three North American ptarmigan species, the willow is found at lower elevations – at or near the timber line, on the tundra where shrub growth dominates, and in boggy openings in the forest and along streams. As the name implies, most of the bird's diet is made up of willow buds.

Early season hunting consists mostly of singles and small coveys, but with the approach of winter the birds begin to gather in larger flocks of two dozen or more.

The willow ptarmigan is also known as the willow partridge, willow grouse, snow grouse and arctic grouse.

RIGHT: The bright red comb is the most readily identified difference between male (on right) and female willow ptarmigan.

Rock ptarmigan

LAGOPUS MUTUS

BELOW: Like all ptarmigan species, this rock ptarmigan goes through seasonal changes in its plumage. This is the summer coat.

About a dozen North American subspecies are commonly known as rock ptarmigan throughout their range, which occurs a bit farther north than that of the willow ptarmigan. Like their cousins, rock ptarmigans migrate to lower elevations and areas of more shelter with the approach of winter each year, although they tend to do this earlier than the willow ptarmigan because of their more northerly location.

The rock ptarmigan is a bit smaller than its southern cousins, with males averaging 12–15 inches in length and weighing no more than one-and-a-quarter pounds. While they share the white winter plumage of the willow ptarmigan in the colder, snowier months of the year, the summer feathers of the male carry a less reddish tint than those of the willow ptarmigan. In winter plumage, the male rock ptarmigan also sports a black line from eye to beak.

The habits of the rock ptarmigan are similar to those of the willow ptarmigan, but the species are found more often in areas of thinner cover and on rocky slopes. Their diet tends more towards catkins and birch buds.

White-tailed Ptarmigan

LAGOPUS LEUCURUS

The smallest of North America's ptarmigan, the white-tailed, rarely travels as far south as the tree line, unlike its two southerly cousins. It is well equipped to withstand even the harshest of winter conditions. However, there are limited populations as far south as Washington and Colorado.

Males are about a foot in length and weigh less than a pound, usually about three-quarters of a pound. Summer plumage is brown with various bars and mottling of black above, and light brown below. The female has a gray to yellow tint, and is the only ptarmigan female to sport a comb. Both have white tails and wings year-round, and are snow white in their winter plumage with black eyes, beaks and claws.

White-tailed ptarmigan are more frequently found on the most barren of rocky slopes, far from the nearest timber line, than are either of their cousins. Adapted to this sparser habitat, they tend to flush at greater distances and fly further than either of the other two species.

The diet of the white-tailed ptarmigan is based on the limited options of its environment, such as mosses, heath and willow.

Locally, the bird is also known as the snow grouse, whitetail, snow partridge and mountain quail.

ABOVE: The white-tailed ptarmigan is the northernmost of all North American ptarmigans. Except for limited populations in Washington and Colorado, it rarely lives below the tree line.

Bobwhite quail

COLINUS VIRGINIANUS

Knowledge of the whereabouts of long-established coveys is the surest way to find bobwhite quail in good numbers. A covey generally claims only a couple dozen acres as its range. But, barring such inside information, which is often a closely guarded secret by those in the know, an understanding of the small bird's needs is the surest route to some fast gunning.

Agricultural fields are needed for food, unless the area is unusually well-supplied with wild seed sources. Beggarweed, ragweed, blackberry, sumac, partridgepea and crabgrass are just some of the wild plants that the bobwhite eats, while wheat, soybean and corn are domestic plants regularly on the diet. Agricultural fields also fulfill the daily need for dust baths and resting. Water is mandatory, and irrigated fields are a boon in the drier reaches of the bird's range. From early winter into mid-spring, the bobwhite also needs relatively thick brushlands for resting and escape.

The bobwhite quail is a very popular game-bird throughout its range, which is generally

LEFT: The location of long-standing bobwhite quail coveys are often closely guarded secrets.

ABOVE: A setter freezes in its track as it spots a hiding bobwhite quail.

limited by harder winters at its northern extreme. Although the bird prospered and flourished with the early development of the continent by man, more recent farming practices and the suburban development of wild areas has hit the overall population hard.

Easily raised under "pen" conditions, the species is common on private hunting preserves and has been introduced into new regions, notably the Pacific Northwest.

The bobwhite is a small gamebird, with males averaging no more than 11 inches in length and a half-pound in weight. Plumage is mottled brown, ranging from reddish to grayish. The bill is short, conical and black. The legs are yellow. Males have a white face, parted by a black streak beak to neck. Females replace the white with buff. There are many subspecies, some of which carry their own distinctive markings.

Although the dogless hunter can meet with some success on this small gamebird, the hunt for the bobwhite quail is primarily a dog sport.

The bird is among the tightest holding of all North American gamebirds, generally flushing at 15 feet or so and then exploding into speeds that quickly reach the 30–50 mile per hour range. A common error is blasting at the birds immediately upon the flush, rather than waiting for them to get airborne and selecting a specific target.

Birds scattered from the covey will usually stay completely still and quiet for 15 to 30 minutes, and then begin whistling to one another and moving to regroup. After the initial flush of the covey it is often best to wait this period of time before going after the singles, unless the exact spot where one has settled has been marked.

BELOW: A hunter and his dogs snap to alert amid a flushing covey of bobwhite quail.

California quail

LOPHPRTYX CALIFORNICUS

Closely related to the Gambel's quail, which it closely resembles, the California quail prefers to run or fly very low over its brushy habitat rather than flushing high into the air. Also known as the valley quail, this is the swiftest of the plumed quail species.

The California quail's most noticeable difference in appearance from the Gambel's is its buff-colored belly scaled in black, similar to that of the scaled quail. In addition, the hen's plume is brownish.

The California quail's range, from southern British Columbia south through the Pacific states, is covered by eight subspecies. Man's introduction of the species has extended its range eastward as well. At the same time, habitat loss has impacted the species in its historical range. It remains the primary upland gamebird of California.

Valley floors, oak-covered foothill slopes and upland chaparral areas are all part of the species' habitat. The bird tends to roost in low trees or brush, rather than on the ground, and feed in relatively open areas rather than the brushy areas where they seek cover. Often individuals can be spotted along dirt roads, picking grit.

Principal food sources are filaree, turkey mullein, barley, clover, lupine, deervetch, oak, thistle and pigweed.

ABOVE: The California quail is the fastest flying of the plumed quail species, but generally prefers running to flight.

Gambel's quail

LOPHORTYX GAMBELII

Also commonly known as the desert quail, this small, plumed bird inhabits the dry regions of the American Southwest with limited populations reaching northeast as far as Colorado. Showing the common quail-family need for water, the bird is most often found near river valleys.

RIGHT: In its hot desert habitat the Gambel's quail is most often active during the early morning and late afternoon into evening.

Like the closely related California, or valley quail, the Gambel's quail most often chooses to run or glide low over the cover rather than take full flight in a flushing burst. After running, the covey will flush at too great a distance for shotgunning. They may hold a bit tighter on subsequent approaches. The one primary exception to this rule takes place when the birds are startled from their midday roost.

The male averages less than a half-pound in weight and no more than 11 inches in length. It is brown to gray with a buff belly that bears a black patch. The head is mostly black, with white borders and the two-pronged plume sprouting from the forehead. The female shares the same body colors, although without the black belly patch. She also has a greatly reduced plume.

Principal wild food sources include mesquite, deervetch, lupine and mustard. Agricultural fields located within a covey's range will also supply some of the bird's diet.

Drought and man's impact on the bird's habitat has reduced populations in recent decades.

Mountain quail

OREORTYX PICTUS

The mountain quail is the largest of this continent's quail species, with males weighing more than a half-pound and measuring as much as a foot in length. Among the plumed quails, it also tends to flush much higher over the landscape. It tends to run to the nearest ridge before flushing.

Spring through late summer finds the mountain quail in the more elevated reaches of its range, but the bird moves into lower, more sheltered habitat similar to that of the Gambel's quail as Fall approaches. However, the ranges of the two species do not overlap much at all and they are rarely found together. The mountain quail occurs in the Pacific states and only slightly east into the Southwest.

Lupine, clover, bromegrass, deervetch and filaree are important food sources, but the mountain quail is often found in oak areas.

Gray-brown with white patches on the belly and rump, the mountain quail has a plume of two black feathers that stands straight up from the bird's head when it is on the ground and arches back over the head when in flight. The male's throat is dark chestnut, bordered with white.

Scaled quail

CALLIPEPLA SQUAMATA

LEFT: Scaled quail tend to gather in increasingly large coveys from early fall into winter. Groups of more than a hundred birds have been reported.

Flushes of scaled quail tend to produce more birds as the season wears on, as the birds congregate for winter. Coveys have been reported at more than 100 birds. The groups stay together until late winter, when pairing begins in preparation for mating.

to the fleeting birds or shoot one of the covey to frighten the rest into flight. Often this results in a flush well out of shotgun range and at speeds ranging up to 35 miles per hour. Sometimes they come back to earth after only a short distance. At other times they glide well beyond the ridge and land on the run.

The bird weighs less than a half-pound and is about a foot in length. The name, cottontop, arises from the pointed, white crest atop the bird's head. Distinctive scaling covers the gray breast and back. A dark line runs through the eye, but the gray head is otherwise unbroken.

Scaled quail occupy more barren habitat than the other quail species that share its Southwest US range. Rocky areas with cacti and thorny shrubs are prime locations. They have a higher tolerance for limited water availability than others of the family, but will congregate at steady water sources.

Wild privet, sorghum, deervetch, pigweed and catclaw are among the primary food sources of the species.

BELOW : The Mearn's quail is also known as the harlequin quail because of the bright coloration of the male, on right.

ABOVE: Scaled quail in mouth, a golden retriever returns with its master's downed prize.

One of the most limited species, in terms of North American range, is the Mearns or harlequin quail, which occurs more abundantly south of the US-Mexican border. However, it does range as far north as Arizona and has been transplanted elsewhere with some success.

About the size of a bobwhite quail, the Mearns is dark gray with many round spots of buff, cinnamon and white appearing throughout except on the unmarked brown breast. The bird follows much the same habits in holding and flushing as the bobwhite.

American woodcock

PHILOHELA MINOR

The woodcock has been in serious decline throughout most of its range for several years, a victim of man's destruction of the bird's moist woodland habitat. So depressed are populations that many avid woodcock hunters are now passing up opportunities to shoot the bird.

It is a strange-looking, chunky bird with a long bill that makes up a full quarter of its 12-inch length, and short, stubby legs. The mottled brown, buff, gray, black and white bird is very well camouflaged for its woodland habitat.

Short, round wings make a whistling noise when the bird flushes, startling the unsuspecting hunter. Though on such occasions the bird flies away in a nearly straight line, its quick jump-start seemingly from nowhere serves the bird well. An able pointing dog helps the hunter to increase his percentage of "hits."

The woodcock occurs east of the Mississippi River and north only so far as southern Canada. The migratory birds follow three primary routes south and north each year: One along the Mississippi River Valley, another along the western edge of the Appalachian Mountains and a third

LEFT : The woodcock is extremely well-camouflaged for its damp woodlands habitat, and a sighting of any bird that remains still is very rare.

be closest to the surface, therefore, have the greatest attraction for the bird: soft, moist earth; tall shrubs and small trees that grow tight to screen out much of the sunlight, with relatively light shrub-covering on the ground.

Prime locations will attract birds repeatedly, offering shooting year in, year out. However as the trees and shrubs grow, allowing more sunlight into the habitat and drying it up, the birds will cease to appear.

Flushes often involve two birds, but these are not a mated pair as is commonly believed. They are just as likely to be two males or two females. And, it's even more likely that at least one of the two will get away scot-free.

Most woodcock are taken over dogs, which make the locating of the scattered and, at times, tight-holding birds an easier task. Those birds bagged by the dogless hunters are most often taken by chance encounter.

BELOW: Woodcock populations are in decline throughout the bird's range. Many ardent woodcock hunters are now passing up shots at the bird to help it recover.

Wild turkey

MELEAGRIS GALLOPAVO

The wild turkey carries a well-deserved reputation as a crafty, wary gamebird, a reputation that is growing as the bird comes under increasingly intense pressure from more and more hunters.

Although many young birds are taken each year by hunters who chance upon them while hunting for other game, the older longbeards generally fall to those who spend their time in careful pursuit. Calling from concealment is the method of choice and spring gobbler seasons have been created to take advantage of the mating urges in the bird.

The turkey has incredible eyesight, able to detect a hunter's presence at great distances, even if that hunter remains perfectly motionless. Its sense of hearing is equally acute.

All wild turkeys of North America are of one species, although there are four different geographic races or subspecies which are distinctly recognizable. Adaptations among the races to have led to the physical differences.

The eastern subspecies (*Meleagris gallopavo silvestris*), which ranges from northern Florida into Canada and west into eastern Texas, is the most widespread and abundant.

ABOVE: From his hiding place, an Indiana shotgunner fires at the turkey that he has called into range.

LEFT: Variety in turkey-hunting equipment has boomed in recent years, as more has been learned about the bird. Shown here is just a small sampling of the many calls that are available on the market today.

LEFT: A tom Rio Grande turkey displays its full regalia. Such displays are used in attracting mates in the spring.

BOTTOM LEFT: The Merriam turkey, or Rocky Mountain turkey, is the West's version of the crafty and intelligent bird.

FACING PAGE: In winter turkey flocks are relatively easy to attract to food and feeders placed within their range.

The Merriam (*Meleagris gallopavo merriami*), also known locally as the Rocky Mountain turkey, is found from Wyoming south to the US-Mexican border and from Arizona east to Texas.

Easterns and Merriams are the largest of the races, with gobblers weighing from 16 to 20 pounds and hens from eight to 12.

The smallest race, both in physical size and in range, is the Osceola or Florida (*Meleagris gallopavo osceola*), which occurs only in Florida.

Rio Grande (*Meleagris gallopavo intermedia*) turkeys dominate in Texas and range, in smaller numbers, north into Oklahoma and Kansas.

All races share the characteristic beard of stiff, hanging hairs protruding from the upper breast of adult males, and some females. In older adult toms this beard is nine inches or longer. It is much shorter in younger toms and usually non-existent in hens.

The adult tom's head and neck are mostly pinkish, marked with some light blue, particularly at the face. The pink is replaced by deep red when the tom struts before hens. Wattles hang from his chin and throat, as do fatty carbuncles further down the neck. The head of the hen has a blue-gray cast because of a coating of thin feathers. The skin of her neck is likewise less brilliant than that of the tom.

The general plumage coloring of all four subspecies is a copper-bronze with black margins, although the irridescent feathers can reflect anything from red-brown to green. There is limited white tipping on the wing feathers. Hens are generally duller than toms.

The above description holds for the eastern race and for the other three, with a few exceptions. The Merriam's tail feathers are tipped in buff, while those of the Rio Grande are tipped in rust. The Osceola tends to have less white on its wings.

During the settlement of the continent by Europeans, all of the races – but most drastically the eastern – suffered a cataclysmic population decline and disappeared from much of their his-

toric ranges. Over-hunting for food and market played a part in this, but loss of their woodland habitat was the primary cause.

Reintroduction efforts across the country – largely in response to the immense popularity of the turkey as a gamebird – have brought the turkey populations back. We still don't have as many turkeys as the continent did in pre-settlement days, but we are definitely better off than at the turn of the century.

Turkeys are naturally a flocking species, and the largest flocks occur in early fall. Those flocks, which can number several dozen, break into smaller flocks – by sex – in early winter.

The big bird is a strong and swift runner, generally preferring that means of escape over flight. It can run at more than 15 miles per hour. When it does take to the air, the turkey flies swiftly but over relatively short distances.

Roosting for the night takes place at about the same time each evening, the set goal being to roost no later than dusk. The flock tends to use the same areas each night, rotating among different trees every few nights when the range offers several roosting alternatives.

Turkey presence in a region is simple to detect, even for the novice outdoorsman. Because of the bird's habit of scratching for its food in the leaf litter over much of its range, a flock of turkeys leaves an unmistakable trail in its wake. A flock at ease also tends to make a lot of clucking and clicking noises among its members. Additionally, a flock will maintain a regular daily schedule, moving through the same area at nearly the same time each day, as long as they are undisturbed by man in this routine.

Turkey with Bacon-Swiss Chard Stuffing

SERVES 6–8

1 wild turkey, dressed

Stuffing:

3 slices bacon

2 tablespoons shallots, chopped

¼ cup chopped celery

¼ pound Swiss chard, chopped

4 cups stale bread cubes

2 eggs, beaten

1½ cups chicken stock

Sauté the bacon in skillet until crisp. Remove and break into small pieces. In the drippings, sauté the shallots and celery. Add Swiss chard and sauté until limp. Cool.

Combine the bacon pieces and shallot/Swiss chard mixture with the bread cubes. Add beaten eggs and enough liquid to moisten thoroughly. Season with pepper, salt if desired. This is a flavorful stuffing that does very well with any game bird. Stuff the turkey and top with bacon slices. Place the bird in a baking pan and cover with a tent of foil. Bake at 450°F.

About 45 minutes before it is done, remove the foil and return the bird to the oven to brown. Baste frequently from this point on. Remove pan juices and prepare gravy to taste.

(ELOISE GREEN, NEW MEXICO WILDLIFE, ALAMOGORDIO DAILY NEWS)

Common crow

CORVUS BRACHYRHYNCHOS

Only a relative handlful of North America's hunters have discovered the wiley adversary that is the common crow, and as a result the large black bird is among the most under-hunted game-birds in North America. Perhaps the fact that, until recently, there were few restrictions on harvesting the crow – which was viewed as a varmint – contributed to this low esteem among much of the hunting fraternity. Federal regulations now classify the bird as migratory and apply seasons to it.

However, the crow can display an incredible ability to learn and adapt to almost everything that the hunter can throw at him. Hunted twice in the same spot, the surviving members of the flock probably will stay outside of shotgun range. Hunted over ground-based decoys, the crows will insist on decoys in the trees as well on the next go-round. On its swooping attack, the bird can reach speeds of as much as 30 miles per hour.

Well-camouflaged hunters, complete with headnets and gloves, conceal themselves in the brush next to a field or large forest opening with decoys – several crows and an owl – scattered in front of them. The electronic or mouth-caller begins cawing.

As the first crows zip into range they must be downed immediately and quickly hidden from sight. These are the scouts. If any or all of them make it back to the rest of the flock, they will warn of the danger and no more of that flock will appear.

At times, it is also effective to allow all of the

RIGHT: Crows that were called into a decoy set-up by hunters flash through the area, some falling to the hunter's gunfire.

LEFT: The crow is more often viewed as a scavenging nuisance rather than the intelligent game bird it really is.

scouts to return to report on the menacing owl that is already under attack by some of their cronies (the decoys). If this is the plan, absolutely none of the scouts must be shot and no hint of the presence of humans must be revealed to them.

During the fall migration period, large arrays of crow decoys – without the owl – can attract migrants to what they believe to be gathering flocks.

A promising site for either of the decoy set-ups is slightly to one side of the flight route of a resident flock, between roosting and feeding areas, or between two feeding areas. Flocks generally travel these routes to feed in the morning, to roost in the early afternoon and again to feed during the early evening. Cornfields are prime feeding sites, but all of man's grain crops are attractive to the birds.

Nearly everyone can identify the common crow, although the smaller fish crow and the larger raven do cause some confusion. The common, or American, crow measures between 16 and 20 inches, from powerful beak to squared tail, and weighs a couple of pounds. It is completely black, except for a reddish tint in the eyes.

The crow occurs in most habitats, except the highly arid, across most of the United States and the southern half of Canada. Cities, suburbs, small towns, agricultural areas, woodlands, wetlands and wilderness all have their populations. Although most Canadian flocks and those in the US Great Plains do migrate southward late each fall, most of the US population is less migratory, moving only a few hundred miles or not at all. In most parts of the country, there are good populations available year round.

Chapter 5

WATERFOWL

While enthusiasts of every form of hunting are generally ready to defend the attractions of their own particular pursuit, it is waterfowl hunting – or waterfowling – that must rank as truly unique.

It is one of our more demanding types of hunting. Bitter, icy, rain-filled mornings that might cause many of us drylanders to linger over that second cup of coffee will find the ardent waterfowler already in the blind. A minimum of specialized equipment is practically mandatory for enjoyment of the sport.

Waterfowling is also demanding because it requires particularly swift identification of birds before firing on them. In the face of declining waterfowl populations, the regulations have been designed to protect some species more than others, and often hens more than drakes. But beyond any legal considerations, today's conservation-minded hunter wants to make the right shot for the benefit of resources, and for many a waterfowler that now means passing up some species entirely.

Novices marvel at the identification abilities of some oldtimers, who can report the species and sex of a bird almost the same instant the rest of us can first make it out on the horizon. Such ability comes only through many years of on-the-job training, so to speak.

In this identification process, seven characteristics of the birds come into play: the silhouette, the manner in which it flies, its coloring pattern, the sound it makes, how it takes off or lands, the actions of the flock, and the habitat in which it is observed.

Although there is overlap, the flyway in which the bird occurs can also be a clue to its identity.

ABOVE : A well-trained and conditioned retriever is constantly anxious for that leap into icy water to fetch a bird that its master has managed to knock from the air.

LEFT: A duck hunter and his black Labrador retriever wait anxiously in an Arkansas swamp, their eyes scanning the skies for incoming targets.

ABOVE: A small flock of tundra swans fly past the autumn moon.

Flyways are those migration routes that large numbers of waterfowl use regularly to travel between nesting and wintering grounds. The four North American flyways are: Atlantic (along the coast and inland), Mississippi (along the River Valley and its drainage), Central (on the eastern side of the Rocky Mountains) and Pacific (along the coast and east to the western side of the Rockies).

It is beyond the scope of this book to provide a detailed course in waterfowl identification. Hour upon hour of field work with binoculars in one hand and a field guide in the other is the means to mastery. In this chapter we will instead offer an overview of the many species of waterfowl that inhabit the continent.

It should also be said that nothing in this book is intended as an encouragement to hunt and shoot one species or another. This is particularly true of waterfowl. No one can dispute the fact that our waterfowl populations are in serious trouble, and many long-time waterfowlers have taken a break for several years at this point to allow the resource to replenish itself.

"With duck populations remaining near all-time lows, the Department of the Interior's US Fish and Wildlife Service has proposed to continue restrictive hunting regulations this fall, Service Director John Turner announced today," began a press release that crossed my desk as I was putting the finishing touches to this book.

"The Service has projected a fall flight index of 64 million ducks, about the same as last year and the third lowest figures since the Service began making such projections in 1969.

Duck numbers fell to record lows during the 1980s as a result of severe drought in prairie nesting areas and continued destruction of wetlands across the continent."

Such pessimistic reports must weigh heavily on every one of us in the hunting fraternity. While the causes of the drastic situation may have been largely beyond our control, perhaps we can be part of the solution.

Voluntary restraint from duck hunters has been urged for several years by the North American Wildlife Foundation. "Let the hens pass, and take satisfaction in being out on the marsh by bringing home a duck or two, instead of the legally allotted daily limit," said Charles S. Potter Jr, executive vice president of the foundation. "The opportunity exists for duck hunters to return the females to the prairies. This represents our potential for a duck recovery."

Beyond practicing restraint, however, those who decide not to hunt ducks at all until the populations rebound should continue to purchase their state, federal and provincial duck stamps. The proceeds from the sale of the stamps is used in vital habitat restoration efforts.

ABOVE: State and federal banding programs across the continent have provided wildlife managers with vital information on many species.

LEFT: On close observation the Canada goose is a very large bird, one factor that leads many a new waterfowler to misjudge the true distance to a passing bird.

TOP Market hunting for many different species has been common at different times across much of North America. Huge kills such as this boatload of ducks taken along Long Island, NY, did great damage to some species' populations. The practice is no longer legal.

Canada goose

BRANTA CANADENSIS

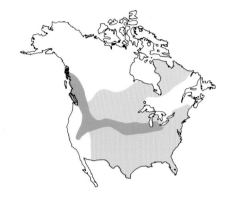

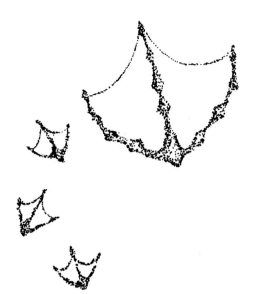

The Canada goose is one of the bright spots on the waterfowl scene. There may actually be more of the big honkers today than ever before. They occur in good numbers across the entire continent. And, while the major high-altitude V-flock migrations continue, many thousands of birds no longer make the flight and remain in their relatively reduced home ranges year-round. City parks and suburban golf courses have been a boon to them.

ABOVE: A trio of hunters prepare their set of silhouette decoys for Canada geese at Middle Creek Wildlife Management Area in central Pennsylvania.

RIGHT: A pair of Canada geese wing their way across the sky. The big birds can reach speeds of up to 60 miles per hour.

Even city dwellers who rarely venture beyond the confines of the concrete jungle can often identify the large mottled gray-brown bird with its long black neck, black head and white patch along the cheek. The several races differ mostly in size, ranging from the smallest at 22 to 26 inches, to the largest at 35 to 45 inches. Weights can range from eight to 20 pounds.

Blinds and decoys – placed in as lifelike position as possible, in grain fields or along waterways frequented by the birds – are the optimum means of taking the birds, accompanied by assorted honks through the goose call.

ABOVE: Amid their set of Canada goose decoys and from the concealment of their pit blind, hunters fire on an incoming flock of the big honkers.

RIGHT: Many hunters wait until the white chin marking can be seen clearly in order to ensure that the Canada goose is within shotgun range. However, the marking can often be seen well beyond the effective range of a shotgun.

Snow goose

CHEN CAERULESCEUS

The three distinct birds that today are considered as snow geese were, until recently, regarded as separate species: the greater snow goose, lesser snow goose and blue goose. More recent investigation has revealed the greater and lesser to be races of the species and the blue to be a color phase of the lesser.

LEFT: Snow geese come in for a landing.

Roast Goose

SERVES 4–6

1 young bird; head, wings, neck, feet removed

salt and freshly ground black pepper

1 teaspoon dried sage

6 cups water

1 onion, sliced

6 whole peppercorns

¼ pound butter, melted

2 tablespoons flour, mixed with ¼ teaspoon garlic powder

Rub the goose with salt and pepper. Sprinkle salt, pepper and the sage into the cavity. Place the bird, breast side up, in a roasting pan. Add 4 cups of water, the onion and peppercorns. Place in a preheated 325°F oven. Roast until the water evaporates. Add the butter and baste the bird.

Roast the goose for 2 more hours, basting regularly. Remove the bird to a heated platter. Stir the flour and garlic mixture into the pan liquid. Add 2 cups water and bring to the boil, reduce the heat and stir until smooth and thickened. Adjust the seasoning and serve the gravy on the side with the goose.

(VICKI SNYDER, FREELANCE OUTDOOR WRITER, COLUMBUS, OHIO)

Lesser snow geese are almost as abundant as the Canada geese, though both races of snow geese are considered better sport than the Canada because of their slightly increased wariness. Snow geese migrate in huge flocks, primarily along the Atlantic and Pacific flyways.

The snow goose ranges from 22 to 30 inches in length and weighs from four to seven pounds. The bird is white with black wing tips. The blue phase, is dark gray with a white neck and head.

LEFT: Camouflaged to blend into the snow-covered landscape of North Dakota, a hunter awaits the approach of a flock of snow geese.

BELOW: Will they turn this way? is the heart-stopping question when a flock of snow geese take to the air in the distance.

Emperor goose

PHILACTE CANAGICA

Relatively few of these birds are taken by hunters, both because of their reluctance to come in to calls or decoys and because of their tendency to avoid areas normally frequented with blinds. In addition, these geese generally winter farther north than prime waterfowling areas, reaching only as far south as the northern California coast. Pass shooting from boats offers the best chance for success.

The Emperor goose is about 24 inches long and weighs from five to seven pounds. It is silvery-gray, often yellowish, with a pink to purplish bill.

RIGHT: Hidden in his grass-camouflaged sneak boat, a hunter calls to a flock of geese in the distance.

White-fronted goose

ANSER ALBIFRONUS

Ross' goose

CHEN ROSSII

The white-fronted goose is more common over the western flyways, on which they often migrate at night. This species commonly mixes with flocks of other species and is taken through the same hunting methods.

Between 26 to 30 inches long and weighing five or six pounds, it is gray-brown with a white belly and patch across the front of the face.

The tule goose is a larger race of the white-fronted, found primarily along the Pacific Flyway. It has been known to be as long as 40 inches and to weigh as much as eight pounds.

This is the smallest of all the wild geese on the continent, measuring no more than 24 inches in length and weighing only two to three pounds. It might be described as a duck-sized version of the snow goose, because the coloring is similar. The Ross' goose also have a rounder head and stubbier bill. Most of this species is found in the Pacific flyway, although some do show up almost each year in the East.

The Ross' goose tends to be less wary of man and is generally more approachable than the other wild goose species. For this reason it was hunted to the brink of extinction by market hunters before it came under federal protection. The population has recovered somewhat and limited hunting is permitted in some areas.

LEFT: White-fronted geese readily mix in with flocks of other species and, as often as not, are taken incidentally to those other species.

ABOVE: Ross' geese in the past were relatively unwary birds that attracted market hunters, who nearly shot the species to extinction. Federal protection has helped the population to recover.

Brant goose

BRANTA BERNICLA

Looking much like a small Canada goose, the brant is a bird of the maritimes. It is rarely found far from the coast and during most of the day rests well out on the ocean. Hunters generally connect with the bird during low tide, when it flies to the eelgrass flats to feed on its preferred food.

When disease destroyed most of these underwater plants earlier this century, the brant population plummeted. But with the comeback of the vegetation came a resurgence of the bird as well. It is now a relatively common species along both coasts.

The brant is 22 to 30 inches long and weighs two-and-a-half to four-and-a-quarter pounds. It is dark brown with a black neck and head.

BELOW: Brant are easily decoyed into range by movement, even the waving of a handkerchief through an opening in the blind.

Stuttgart Betty's Roast Mallard

SERVES AS DESIRED

Any number of dressed, whole mallards
(or other ducks)

salt

baking soda

onions

green bell peppers

celery

flour

milk (optional)

Salt the ducks to taste and rub with baking soda. Allow them to sit 1 hour, then wash off the soda. Stuff the body cavity of each bird with small chunks of onion, bell pepper and celery, then rub the birds with flour. Place in a large roasting pan with enough water to half-cover the ducks. Cook in a preheated 350°F oven for 3 to 3½ hours, or until the birds are tender. Remove the vegetable stuffing and discard. Halve each bird lengthwise before serving. If desired, thicken the broth from the ducks with a milk and flour mixture to make gravy. Serve birds on a bed of rice.

(DEVELOPED AT HARTZ DUCK CAMP IN STUTTGART, ARKANSAS; SUBMITTED BY KEITH SUTTON, FREELANCE OUTDOOR WRITER, BENTON, ARK.)

BELOW RIGHT: Mallards are the most familiar of all duck species.

RIGHT: The brilliant green head of the mallard drake can be seen for considerable distances.

Mallard duck

ANAS PLATYRHYNCHOS

The mallard is a familiar bird to almost everyone; in fact it is North America's most common duck. It is common on all flyways and will winter as far north as it can locate ice-free water.

In the early morning and late afternoon, the mallard flock alights from the body of water where it has spent the night and midday, and moves to grain fields or flooded woodlands for feeding.

The bird is 17 to 27 inches long and weighs two to three pounds. Males are light gray with deep tan breasts, green heads and white neck rings. Females are brown with white tails.

Pintail duck
ANAS ACUTA

Found in all flyways, the pintail is another common waterfowl species. It is capable of very fast flight, and often swoops from considerable heights just before landing.

This species is among the most popular of North American game birds for its flying ability, wariness of man and tasty meat.

Both sexes average between about 21 to 30 inches long and weigh one-and-a-half to two pounds. The male is a patterned maze of black and white lines on the sides and onto the back, with steel gray feathers towards the rear. The head is olive brown with a blue bill. The female is pale gray-brown with white at the back of her head.

LEFT: Combining an overall wariness of man with pleasing taste on the table, the pintail is among the most popular duck species.

BOTTOM LEFT: Surrounded by their decoys, a pair of hunters pepper the skies as a flock of ducks flies by.

Vern's Duck Fingers
SERVES 2

2 duck breasts
2 eggs, slightly beaten
1 cup milk
salt and freshly ground black pepper
cracker meal (no substitutes)
vegetable oil (enough for ½-inch depth
in skillet)

Fillet the duck breasts. Slice fillets crosswise into ¼-inch-wide strips. Salt and pepper lightly.
Combine milk and eggs in a shallow bowl. Dip duck strips into the mixture, then roll them in cracker meal. Fry in batches in hot oil until golden brown. Drain on paper towels.

(DEVELOPED BY VERNON BAKER, NORTH LITTLE ROCK, ARKANSAS;
SUBMITTED BY KEITH SUTTON, FREELANCE OUTDOOR WRITER, BENTON, ARK.)

Black duck

ANAS RUBRIPES

A duck of mostly the Atlantic and Mississippi flyways, the black duck is one of the most skittish and difficult to bag. It is primarily a duck of the large rivers.

Black ducks are 17 to 24 inches long and weigh two-and-a-half to three pounds. The male is brown, scalloped with lighter brown everywhere but on its head. The female is duller and lighter.

ABOVE: A large raft of black ducks rests undisturbed on an isolated pocket of water.

LEFT: Although populations have declined in recent years, the black duck remains among the most common and most sought-after species.

Gadwall duck

ANAS STREPERA

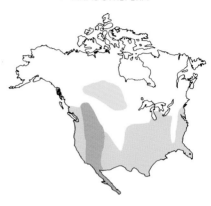

The fast-flying gadwall has the widest range of any duck. It is found along all flyways, since it has become a breeder along the Atlantic Coast .

A flock of gadwalls tends to fly in tight formation with swift wingbeats. The bird is 17 to 20 inches long and weighs one-and-a-half to two-and-a-half pounds. The male is gray with a brown head, black rump and white patch on the rear edge of the wing. The female is brown with the same wing patch.

ABOVE: A male gadwall moves in front of a flock of mallards. Gadwalls, generally among the least wary of ducks, are taken both over decoys and in jump shots.

Wood duck

AIX SPONSA

Commonly known as the woodie, the wood duck drake is the handsomest waterfowl on the continent. He is covered in a distinctive pattern of iridescent blues, greens and purples, with outlines of white, a chin patch of white and a long red bill. His mate is mostly gray-brown with a white eyering. Both are between 13 and 20 inches long and weigh one-and-a-quarter to one-and-a-half pounds.

The species is most often located on slow-moving streams, backwaters and flooded woodlands. As this type of habitat has dwindled across the bird's range, so has the population of woodies, though it is still found along all flyways except the Central.

BELOW: The wood duck is a bird of the forested swamp and flooded woodlands, quite willing and able to forage for its food on the forest floor.

Blue-winged teal

ANAS DISCORS

A close relative of the shoveler, the blue-winged teal shares the former's habit of early migration but not its poor taste. This small species is actually considered excellent fare.

Although it is not uncommon along any of the flyways, it is most numerous on the potholes and ponds of the central continent.

The blue-winged teal flies in small, swift flocks, which generally move through wooded areas as though they were one bird.

Between 14 and 16 inches in length, this teal weighs less than a pound. The male is brown, dotted with black, with a light blue shoulder patch and a white vertical band in front of each eye. The female is gray-brown with same shoulder patch.

BELOW: Blue-winged teal are easily decoyed into range, as they spend a great deal of the day moving about a given area in search of food.

Northern shoveler

ANAS CLYPEATA

This spoon-billed species is much more common along the Central and Pacific flyways, where it is among the earliest migrators, north and south, of all waterfowl. Stagnant ponds are the common habitat of the shoveler.

ABOVE: The shoveler's huge bill has given rise to many common names for the species, including shovelmouth, spoonbill, broadface and broadbill.

RIGHT: Because of their tendency to feed by filtering mud through their bills in search of their food, the meat of shovelers is generally held to be among the least edible of all ducks.

Many waterfowlers consider it among the least suitable of waterfowl for table fare, as the flesh tends to take on the taste of its primarily crustacean diet. Its habit of bottom-feeding also makes the shoveler susceptible to botulism.

The shoveler's most noticeable feature is the large bill, which gives it its name. The duck ranges from 16 to 20 inches in length and weighs about a pound. The male has a white body, tan sides and a green head. The female is mottled brown with light blue patches on the wings.

Green-winged teal

ANAS CRECCA

The green-winged teal is seen along all four flyways, but most commonly along the Pacific and Central. One of the latest migrators, it is another species that tends to winter as far north as it can find open water.

It is among the fastest of all waterfowl, traveling in large, tight flocks. These are often conspicuous for their elaborate mid-air manuevers.

Marshy lakes and ponds are the bird's preferred habitat.

The green-winged teal is 12 to 17 inches long and weighs about three-quarters of a pound. The male has a reddish brown head with an iridescent green band, patterned gray and white sides, some tan wing feathers and a white rump. The female is deep brown.

RIGHT: Green-winged teal often seem almost anxious to come into decoys, continuing to fly past sets even after shots have been fired at them.

Cinnamon teal

ANAS CYANOPTERA

BELOW LEFT: The cinnamon teal is found in its greatest numbers in the western half of the continent.

A bird of the Pacific and Central flyways, cinnamon teal are often found among smaller flocks of their blue-winged cousins, in areas where the two species' range overlap. The cinnamon teal, however, tends not to appear in large flocks. Without examination of the internal organs it is nearly impossible to distinguish the hens of the two species. Both share the habit of early migration.

The cinnamon teal is not easily flushed. It is generally slow to take flight from the prairie marshlands and reed-lined streams that it inhabits.

The bird is 14 to 16 inches in length and weighs less than a pound. The male is shimmering brown on the sides and face, and gray-brown across the back. The female is light brown with light blue patches on the wings.

Canvasback duck

AYTHYA VALISINERIA

ABOVE RIGHT: Canvasbacks generally rank among the tastiest of duck species.

The canvasback is another species particularly hard hit by the continuing declines in duck populations across North America. Although it is generally considered among the best eating duck species, many waterfowlers currently are passing it up. Another fortunate aid to its survival is the fact that the canvasback is a wary, cautious bird, demanding the utmost care in preparation by the hunter.

The species breeds mainly in the West, but can be found along all four flyways of the continent. "Cans," as they are commonly known, tend to fly in fast-moving V-shaped flocks.

The canvasback is 18 to 24 inches long and weighs as much as three pounds. The male is white with a red-brown head and a black chest. The female is gray-brown. Both have a long bill and a sloping profile to their head.

Redhead duck

AYTHYA AMERICANA

A regular traveling companion of the canvasback, the redhead has suffered a similarly serious population decline, largely through habitat loss. Today it is probably one of the least common ducks in North America.

The species is often seen in large flocks – known as rafts – floating in deep water areas, where they spend most of the day at rest. Redheads tend to feed mostly at night.

The duck is 17 to 23 inches long and weighs two to two-and-a-half pounds. The male is gray with a black breast and red head. The female is brownish-gray. Both have a light blue bill and a gray stripe on the wing.

Ring-necked duck

AYTHYA COLLARIS

LEFT: The redhead tends to settle on large bodies of water, such as bays or lakes.

Seen mostly along the Atlantic, Mississippi and Pacific flyways, the ring-necked duck tends to inhabit wooded lakes and ponds much more frequently than other diving ducks.

The duck is 15 to 18 inches long and weighs between one-and-a-half and one-and-three-quarter pounds. The male is black, with a purplish sheen on the head, white sides and belly, and gray tail. The black bill has a white band at its base and near the tip. The female is brown with a white ring around each eye.

RIGHT: The drake of the misnamed ring-necked duck species sports white rings on its bill and at the base of the bill but no such rings around its neck.

American widgeon

ANAS AMERICANA

Also commonly known as the baldpate, the American widgeon is found along all four flyways. It is an easily flushed bird that takes off and flies in an erratic, twisting fashion.

It is often found among flocks of diving ducks, from whom the widgeon steals the food when the latter surfaces. Grainfields and meadows also attract this adaptable bird, which grazes like a goose.

The American widgeon is 17 to 23 inches long and weighs less than two pounds. The male is brown with a white crown, green band on the head and white patches on the shoulders. The female is brown with a gray head and the same white shoulder patches.

ABOVE: The American widgeon is commonly found amid flocks of diving ducks, stealing the food that the other species retrieve from the bottom.

European widgeon

ANAS PENELOPE

Although far from common on American shores, enough examples of this European cousin of the American widgeon are beginning to show up in the flocks of its New World cousin – along both coasts – to warrant a mention here.

Like the American widgeon, the European variety is a wary bird that is quick to take flight and is generally considered a top gamebird in its European homelands.

The European widgeon is 17 to 21 inches long and weighs one-and-a-half to one-and-three-quarter pounds. The male has a red-brown head with a tan crown and a gray body. The female is brown. Both sexes have a blue bill.

Bufflehead duck

BUCEPHALA ALBEOLA

These smallest of the diving ducks are common along all flyways, and particularly in winter along both coasts. There it travels in small flocks rather than in large rafts like much of its kin.

Commonly referred to as the butterball, the bufflehead is a late migrator. In flight it tends to cruise close to the surface of the water, with swift wingbeats.

The bird is 14 to 19 inches long and weighs about a pound. The male has a purplish-black back and front half of its head, and a white belly, breast, and rear half of its head. The female is light gray, paler on the belly and breast, with a white cheek patch.

BOTTOM LEFT: The bufflehead generally is not found on a waterfowler's list of most desirable species for the table. Its meat often has a very strong taste.

Ruddy duck

OXYURA JAMAICENSIS

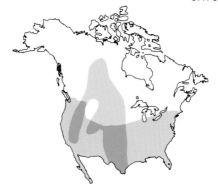

Found along all flyways, the ruddy duck is not much of a gamebird. It is reluctant to fly and prefers instead to dive underwater or hide among the marsh grasses to escape danger.

It generally appears to have a tough time taking to the air, but once there is a strong, fast flier.

The ruddy duck is about 15 to 17 inches long and weighs about a pound. The male has a tan body, white cheek patches and a black crown, plus a blue bill during the mating season. The female is dull brown, with white cheek patches. Both sexes tend to hold their tails erect while on the water.

BELOW: The ruddy duck is easily decoyed into shooting range and generally reluctant to flush when threatened.

Common goldeneye

BUCEPHALA CLANGULA

Also known as the whistler, for the sound its wings make in flight, this larger relative of the bufflehead is found along all four flyways. When frightened, the common goldeneye appears to leap from the water in a series of quick spirals.

The bird is 16 to 21 inches long and weighs one-and-three-quarter to two-and-a-quarter pounds. The male has a white body, black back, and dark green head with a white cheek patch. The female is mottled gray with a brown head.

RIGHT: In flight the wings of the common goldeneye produce a whistling noise from which arises the nickname of "whistler."

Barrow's goldeneye

BUCEPHALA ISLANDICA

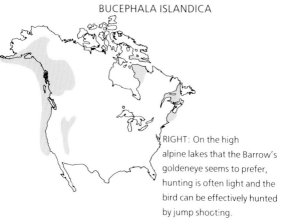

RIGHT: On the high alpine lakes that the Barrow's goldeneye seems to prefer, hunting is often light and the bird can be effectively hunted by jump shooting.

This hardy bird shows a decided preference for high alpine lakes and thus winters far north of most other waterfowl species. It is found primarily along the northern Atlantic and Pacific coasts. Like many ducks, it is a species in decline.

The Barrow's goldeneye is 16 to 19 inches long and weighs between two and three pounds. The male has a black back with white markings at the sides, a purplish tint at the back of the head and the rump, and a white belly, breast, and a white cheek patch. The female is gray-brown, with more brown at the head, and a white collar.

Lesser scaup

AYTHYA AFFINIS

Found along all four flyways, the lesser scaup occurs in large rafts on lakes and on the ocean in the South during the winter. In the North, where the greater scaup is more common, it is found in smaller groups. The birds are usually restless and in constant motion in these rafts.

The species is 16 to 19 inches in length and weighs one-and-a-half to two pounds. The male is gray, with a black chest and a purplish black head. The female is brown, with a white patch on each cheek.

ABOVE: The lesser scaup is a widespread species, found along both coastal and inland waters.

BELOW : A small flock of lesser scaup skim over the Missouri River in North Dakota.

Greater scaup

AYTHYA MARILA

This is a slightly bigger relative of the lesser scaup. It is often encountered in large rafts of several thousand birds, at first on good-sized lakes, before they become ice-covered, and thereafter on saltwater. This trait can generally be used to distinguish between the greater and lesser species in the Northeast.

The greater scaup is a little larger – between 16 and 21 inches long and weighing one-and-three-quarter to two-and-a-half pounds. Otherwise the male is similar, except for the green sheen on its black head, while the female is not easily distinguishable from the female of the other species.

ABOVE: Mollusks make up more than half of the diet of the greater scaup over much of the area where it is hunted in the fall and winter.

American eider

SOMATERIA MOLLISSIMA

It is the down from this species which is largely responsible for the reputation for softness of the eider-down pillow. Into the early 1900s, the American eider was pursued by hunters to near extinction for these valuable feathers. With the end of such market hunting, however, the bird has staged a fairly healthy comeback.

This largest of North American ducks is a hardy bird that rarely migrates far from its nesting grounds and is therefore seldom seen in the continental United States. It occurs along both coasts of Canada and Alaska.

The American eider is 22 to 27 inches long and weighs three-and-a-half to four-and-a-half pounds. The male has a white back, head and breast, and a black crown and belly. The female is shades of brown.

RIGHT: American eider tend to migrate in small flocks over coastal areas, where pass shooting proves successful. Female (left) and male (right) are shown here.

King eider

SOMATERIA SPECTABILIS

This coastal species is rarely seen in the United States, although in its northern habitat it maintains a large population. In North America, it occurs along the eastern and northern coasts of Canada.

Slightly smaller than the American eider, it also tends towards deeper waters and will dive considerable depths to maintain its fish and shellfish diet.

The king eider is 18 to 26 inches long and weighs two to three pounds. The male looks much like the common eider but with a black back and orange mantle on the forehead. The female is similar to the common eider.

Harlequin duck

HISTRIONICUS HISTRIONICUS

Largely a saltwater species, the harlequin moves to inland freshwater streams only for the breeding season. In either habitat, the diet is made up of snails, small fish, crustaceans and saltwater barnacles.

This is another species that tends to remain across the Canadian border, although it is not uncommon along the northern reaches of both US coasts.

The harlequin duck is 14 to 21 inches long and usually weighs less than one-and-a-half pounds. The male has a blue-gray head with white and rust markings, a gray breast, black and white back, rust belly and gray tail feathers that are held erect. The female is brown with white patches on her sides.

RIGHT: Harlequin ducks are not all difficult to decoy into shotgunning range. They will often move in to investigate a raft of decoys of other species.

Surf scoter

MELANITTA PERSPICILLATA

Like most other fish-eaters, the flesh of the surf scoter is generally not regarded very highly. Rafts of the surf scoter are often seen diving for food near the breakwater line. Although it occurs along both coasts, it tends to stay in northerly waters.

The duck is 17 to 21 inches long and weighs two to three pounds. The male is black overall, with a white forehead, a white patch at the back of head and a large orange bill. The female is mottled gray, brown and black.

White-winged scoter

MELANITTA FUSCA

Common scoter

MELANITTA NIGRA

Oldsquaw

CLANGULA HYEMALIS

This species is the largest and most widespread of the North American scoters. It occurs along both coasts.

Like the surf scoter, it is an ocean-going diver. But it tends to occupy deeper water than does the surf scoter. It floats in tight rafts and flies in long lines.

The white-winged scoter is 18 to 24 inches long and weighs between two and four pounds. The male is black, with white on the wings and a large yellow bill. The female is brown, with white patches on the face and wings.

Betrayed by its name, the common scoter is actually the most *uncommon* of the three species in North America. It is also the smallest of the three.

The species is found along the Atlantic and the Pacific coasts, but generally in more northerly waters.

The common scoter is 17 to 21 inches long and weighs between two and three pounds. The male is black, with white patches on the forehead and back of the head, and a large yellow and black bill. The female is dull gray, with off-white cheek patches and black bill.

Unlike most other diving ducks, the oldsquaw actually uses its wings to swim underwater. Because of this, the species is able to dive to much greater depths than most of its peers.

The oldsquaw is common along both coasts, and on some lakes. It is a fast flier, but tends to do most of its flying at night. In spring, it is also a very noisy bird.

The usual length is 15 to 23 inches, and weight one to two pounds. The male oldsquaw is marked in white, gray and black, with a gray cheek/eye patch and long black tail feathers. The female is paler, without the long tail feathers.

LEFT: The oldsquaw is among the most able diving ducks of North America. It can travel surprising distances underwater, using its wings as well as its feet.

Common merganser

MERGUS MERGANSER

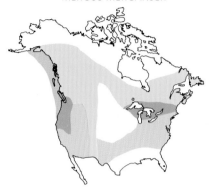

This fish-eater was once heavily persecuted by hunters who were also fishermen in the belief that it ate too many fish and thus damaged the angling sport. However, more recent evidence suggests that the bird actually helps to prevent overpopulation, thus contributing to larger, healthier fish. The persecution has pretty much come to an end.

Because of its diet the common merganser, which occurs in all four flyways, is definitely not among the tastiest of our ducks.

This species measures from 21 to 27 inches in length and weighs about two-and-a-half to four pounds. The male is white, with a green head and a bright red bill. The female is gray, with a brownish head.

TOP LEFT: Although the meat of the hooded merganser definitely cannot be placed among the tastiest of the ducks, it is generally more palatable than that of other mergansers because its diet includes more vegetable matter.

BOTTOM LEFT: A common merganser lands on the water in typical merganser fashion.

Hooded merganser

LOPHODYTES CUCULLATUS

This smallest North American merganser is among the continent's fastest flying ducks. It usually travels in small flocks of no more than a dozen birds, along rivers and estuaries, and is generally not seen along the Central Flyway.

The hooded merganser ranges from 16 to 20 inches in length and weighs about one to one-and-a-half pounds. The male is black with brown sides, a larger "hooded" head that is white, framed in black across the rear half, and a white breast. The female is gray, with a brown head.

Red-breasted merganser

MERGUS SERRATOR

Although the red-breasted merganser is somewhat similar to the common merganser, this species is the only one of the three commonly inhabiting saltwater areas. It is primarily a bird of the Atlantic and Pacific flyways.

The bird is 18 to 25 inches long and weighs between one-and-three quarter and three pounds. The male has black and gray sides, a green head, reddish-brown breast and a white ring around its neck. The female is gray, with a brown head and white breast. Both have crests and red bills.

Swans

CYGNUS SPP

Nearly extinct in the 1930s, the trumpeter swan (*Cygnus buccinator*) has rebounded somewhat. Small but increasing populations now exist in several states along the northern Rockies. This largest of North American waterfowl – 60 to 72 inches long and 25 to 40 pounds in weight – was never overly abundant. It is white, with a black bill that can be seen, at close range, to be framed in pink.

The whistling swan (*Cygnus columbianus*) is seen each fall in large numbers along both coasts. In addition, sizeable numbers make brief stops on the Great Lakes and rivers of that region. It is smaller than the trumpeter, measuring 48 to 56 inches long and weighing 16 to 20 pounds.

The mute swan (*Cygnus olor*) is an introduced species that occurs primarily from New England south through Maryland, and appears to be causing nesting conflicts with some native birds. It is about 52 to 60 inches long and weighs 20 to 30 pounds.

ABOVE: As his mate sits on the clutch of eggs, a male mute swan guards against all intruders, including the photographer who is currently attracting his ire.

RIGHT: The trumpeter swan, which might weigh more than 35 pounds, is the giant among all North American waterfowl.

Roasted Young Swan

SERVES 4–5

1-year-old bird (3½ to 4 pounds dressed)
1 tablespoon flour
3 stalks celery, sliced
salt and freshly ground black pepper
1 teaspoon sage
1 onion, quartered
1 tablespoon vegetable oil
1 teaspoon celery seed

Preheat the oven to 350°F. Shake flour in a large size (14-by-20-inch) oven cooking bag. Place the bag in a large, 2-inch-deep, roasting pan. Add the sliced celery to the bag. Sprinkle the swan cavity with the salt, pepper and sage; place the onion quarters inside. Close the cavity with skewers. Brush breast and legs with oil.

Sprinkle the bird with salt, pepper and the celery seed. Place the swan in the bag and close it with a nylon tie; make 6 half-inch slits in the top.

Cook the swan 1½ hours, or until tender. During the last 15 minutes of cooking, split the bag down the middle and brown the swan at 425°F.

(JOAN CONE, FREELANCE OUTDOOR WRITER, WILLIAMSBURG, VA.)

Chapter 6

WETLAND BIRDS

Rails

RALLINAE

Because they tend to run through the thick marsh grasses rather than fly and – when they do take to the wing, fly slow, straight and low – many hunters look down on rails. Those who have tried the sport, on the other hand, have found it to be a fast-paced pursuit, often offering only fleeting glimpses of the quarry before it slips back into the vegetation.

There are several species across the continent, but only four are generally considered gamebirds. The largest, the sora (*Porzana carolina*), is slightly bigger than a quail. It is also marked much like a bobwhite quail, but with longer legs and a longer, yellow bill. It is found from central Canada, south throughout California in the West, and into Pennsylvania in the East. It also occurs from the Carolinas through Florida.

Ranging throughout the northern half of the United States, south along both coasts and into southern Canada, is the Virginia rail (*Rallus limicola*). It is about quail size, with reddish-brown plumage, marked with black across its body, except for the bright gray at its face and a long red bill.

The king rail (*Rallus eleganus*) is found throughout the eastern half of the United States, south of New England and most of the Great Lakes region. It is similar to the Virginia rail, but larger and with buff rather than gray at the face. Its bill is a paler red.

While the others are primarily birds of the freshwater marsh, the clapper rail (*Rallus longirostris*) is an inhabitant of saltwater wetlands. It

is a long-billed, gray-brown bird that resembles the king rail, but without the rusty underside. It is found along all coasts of the United States.

Most serious rail hunting is done from a boat, with one hunter sitting forward to do the shooting and the other operating the boat from the stern. A swiftly moving boat generally produces more flushes by pushing the birds harder, forcing them into flight rather than a running escape. Multiple flushes are not at all uncommon, although the birds will generally rise from many points in the area rather than from one spot as a flock.

ABOVE: The sora rail is the largest North American member of the rail family. It is about the size of a large bobwhite quail.

RIGHT: The clapper rail is most common through the saltwater estuaries of the southeastern United States.

American coot

FULICA AMERICANA

Often seen feeding amid mixed flocks of ducks in the open, coots are the most water-going members of the *Rallidae* clan. Decoys of the chicken-sized bird are used as a confidence builder by many duck hunters.

But that's where the similarity ends. Coots are much less wary than ducks. They must run along the surface of the water for considerable distances to get airborne. And, like others of their clan, coots prefer to slink into the tall marsh grasses as their primary means of escape.

Coot hunting is done mostly by walking or boating along marshy shorelines, flushing a few birds from the widely scattered flock at a time. Often the birds will swim a distance into open water, possibly out of shotgunning range, before beginning their running/splashing take-off. The birds generally cannot be lured into range by decoy or call.

The bird measures no more than 16 inches in length and weighs only a couple of pounds. It is slate gray to black, with red eyes and a white bill. It is found across nearly all of the United States and southern Canada.

Common gallinule

GALLINULA CHLOROPUS

Purple gallinule

PORPHYRULA MARTINICA

Gallinules are closely related to rails and coots, and they inhabit some of the same range. But gallinules generally do not hide in the thick marsh vegetation as much as rails, nor do they swim in open water as much as coots.

These small birds are not found in true flocks, but often as many as a dozen can be flushed relatively close to one another in the same general feeding area.

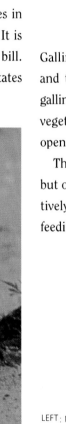

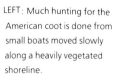

LEFT: Much hunting for the American coot is done from small boats moved slowly along a heavily vegetated shoreline.

Most gallinules are taken secondarily to other species that the hunter has come afield in search of, and many hunters would not even be able to identify the bird. Consequently, it does not feel the impact of a great deal of hunting pressure.

The common gallinule is the more widely distributed of the two species. It can be found in wetlands throughout the eastern half of the United States and in scattered locations in the Southwest.

It is about 12 inches long and weighs less than a pound. It is slate gray, with a yellow-tipped gray bill, red frontal shield and white on the underside of its tail.

The slightly larger purple gallinule – up to 14 inches long and sometimes more than a pound in weight – is found from the Carolinas south through Florida and west through Texas. It is also seen further north, but not in great numbers.

It is iridescent green across its back and sides, purplish blue on its breast, neck and head, with a yellow-tipped red bill and sky blue frontal shield.

LEFT: The chicken-like purple gallinule is most often taken by hunters in search of other game who happen to flush it from its waterside hiding place.

ABOVE: While a few common gallinules may be flushed in the same general area within a few minutes of each other, the bird generally does not form into flocks.

Sandhill crane

GRUS CANADENSIS

Although human development and draining of wetlands has impacted on this large bird's population and greatly reduced its range, it continues to migrate in large flocks from its breeding grounds in the Arctic. Large congregations can still be found at locations such as the Platte River in Nebraska.

During these fall migrations, the cranes feed mostly on agricultural grains, such as corn, wheat and rice, offering hunters ready clues to their presence.

Decoys are effective on the flock-loving birds, provided the hunters are completely hidden and patient enough to wait for just the right moment to take the shot. Sandhill cranes have exceedingly strong eyesight and are very shy of man. Even a car parked nearby is thought by some hunters to be enough to turn the flock and send them winging over the horizon.

Pass shooting from a blind at the birds' roosting waters is also effective, particularly when located between the water and the grain fields where the cranes are feeding. The bird glides at 40 to 50

ABOVE: The sandhill crane is among the shyest of North American game birds and will "spook" at even the slightest hint that something is out of the ordinary.

BELOW: Like some strange creatures from another time, a flock of sandhill cranes are revealed as the fog begins to lift.

miles per hour. On the wintering grounds, action is likely to continue throughout the day.

The sandhill crane stands as tall as four feet and weighs seven to nine pounds. It is gray, mottled with white, buff and brown, and red at the forehead. It has a very long neck and legs, which it holds outstretched in flight.

Breeding grounds are in Alaska, northern Canada, portions of the Rockies, Florida and Siberia, while winter grounds are found along the southern border of the United States.

The protected greater sandhill crane (*Grus canadensis tabida*) is almost identical to the sandhill but much larger. It stands more than four feet tall and weighs about 15 pounds. The greater breeds and winters in other regions, and hunting is generally permitted only in those states that are not host to the larger bird.

Common snipe

CAPELLA GALLINAGO

The common snipe looks much like the wood-cock and shares many of the same habits. However, the snipe is generally found in wetter environments and its food is more often aquatic snails or insect larvae rather than earthworms.

It prefers grassy areas covered with shallow water – except for some tufts and raised areas – mostly enclosed with low brush for escape and hiding cover. Freshwater, saltwater and brackish areas such as these can all hold snipe.

Snipe hunting generally involves walking into the wind along promising wetland areas to put the birds up. Generally they will launch – with a loud rasping cry – into the wind and then fly in that same direction, zigzagging at first but soon straightening out. Once aloft, the snipe will head for the nearest opening in the treeline. A missed bird will often return a short while later to the spot from which it was flushed. The best hunting seems to occur early in the morning, late in the afternoon and on cloudy days.

The snipe is a small bird, always less than a foot in length and weighing less than a pound. It is brown, with lines of black and white across its back, and sports a long brownish bill.

Although it is common for the birds to migrate as flocks during the night, they are most often found as singles during the day.

ABOVE: When flushed, the common snipe launches into the wind in a zigzagging pattern.

Chapter 7

RACCOON AND OPOSSUM

Raccoon

PROCYON LOTOR

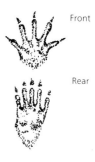

Front

Rear

Crashing through the nighttime woods behind the baying hounds, hot and eager on the fresh trail of a raccoon, is an experience unlike anything else in hunting. It is a series of moments filled with anticipation of the unknown and unexpected. Then the baying becoming more heated; the coon has treed.

RIGHT: The raccoon is a hardy, adaptable animal that can exist abundantly either in the shadow of human habitation, making use of whatever of man's discards it finds, or deep in the forest far from any human.

Shooting the animal is almost anticlimactic, and small individuals are regularly passed up. However, coon meat is very tasty fare and provides ample justification for harvesting the animal.

The coon can also be called into gunning range by a concealed hunter using a predator call, either manual or electronic. The small-bird-in-distress-call appears to be most effective.

The most notable features of the coon are its black bandit mask across the eyes and its black-and-brown horizontally striped tail. Its roundish body is grizzled gray to brown, with its lower legs and feet appearing naked and black. Less than 20 pounds is average for the two to three foot-long animal, although enough 30 pounders are taken every year to make that size not uncommon.

Most hunters associate the coon with watery environments such as small ponds and shallow streams, and the animal is found there frequently, when food like frogs, crayfish and mussels are common. However, the coon is just as likely to be found on ridges and in mountain valleys, in search of berries, wild grapes and nuts.

The raccoon is found throughout most of the United States and southern Canada, except some areas in the Rockies and the Southwest.

Rodent Scat

RIGHT: Hounds bay and hunters gather at the base of a tree where the dogs have "treed" a raccoon.

Barbecued Coon, Arkansas Style

SERVES 4–6

1 raccoon
water
1 large onion, chopped
1 cup chopped celery
salt and freshly ground black pepper
your favorite barbecue sauce

Skin and wash the coon thoroughly, then cut into 6 parts. Cut off all 4 legs, as if you were cutting up a chicken for barbecuing; leg and thigh should be in one piece. The remaining part of the body is simply cut in 2 crosswise. Each of the legs needs to be cut open at the bend in their joint to remove the small white gland. Place the cut-up coon in a large pot of water. Add the onion and celery, then salt and pepper to taste. Bring to a boil, turn the fire down and let simmer until tender. Remove the meat from the pot, arrange on an outdoor grill, and baste with the barbecue sauce. It's best not to have your coals too hot, as the coon is precooked, and you only want the meat to crisp and soak up the flavor of the sauce. Keep turning and basting the coon in the barbecue sauce for another hour. Serve with roasted corn, coleslaw, baked beans and plenty of cold beer.

(KEITH SUTTON, FREELANCE OUTDOOR WRITER, LITTLE ROCK, ARK.)

Opossum

DIDELPHIS MARSUPIALIS

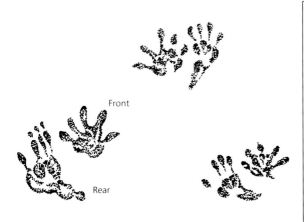

Front

Rear

Commonly referred to simply as the possum, this strange hold-over from centuries past is North America's only marsupial, or pouched mammal. Unlike other mammals, the female carries the young inside her body for only a week or two before they are born in an undeveloped embryonic stage. The tiny, hairless creatures then crawl to the pouch, where they will remain for another two months of development.

The possum is hunted much like the raccoon, with hounds, although the chase is generally much shorter. It usually ends with the possum in a relatively short, heavily-leaved tree. Encountered without dogs, or with just a single dog to act as an opponent, the possum may first try to run to escape, then either play dead or stage bluff attacks.

Adult possums can measure as much as 40 inches in length and weigh nearly 15 pounds, although the average is somewhat smaller. The animal is covered with grizzled dark gray to white fur above, with a paler belly. The face is covered by very short, tight hair that is white to yellowish. The black, pink-tipped ears and the scaley gray-to-white tail are naked.

Most of the eastern United States, as far west as Texas, is home to the possum. There are also populations along the west coast, north into British Columbia.

ABOVE: The opossum is a slow-moving, foul-smelling animal that would just as soon curl in a ball and play dead as run from a hunter.

Roast Possum, Florida Style

SERVES 2–4

1–2 possums, halved
salt and freshly ground black pepper
2–4 bacon strips
2–4 sweet potatoes, peeled
2–4 tart apples, cored

Rub the cleaned possum halves with the salt and pepper and place them, belly side down, in a large roasting pan. Arrange 1 or 2 bacon strips across each piece and pour a little boiling water into the bottom of the pan. Roast at 350°F for 1 hour. Check once or twice and add a little more water, if necessary. At the end of the hour add 1 sweet potato per person. Roast another hour, basting regularly. Add 1 apple per person and bake for 1 more hour, basting frequently. Arrange the potatoes, apples and possum on a platter and drift with freshly minced parsley. Serve with slabs of cornbread with honey butter, cabbage and carrot slaw, a fruity blush wine, and spice cake with caramel frosting.

(JANET GROENE, DELAND, FLA, AUTHOR OF THE BOOKS *COOKING ON THE GO* AND *COOKING ABORAD YOUR RV*)

Chapter 8

CANINES

Red fox

VULPES VULPES

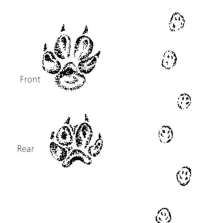

Front

Rear

The reputation for craftiness and elusiveness has not been given to the red fox without some very good reasons. This small canine can elude entire packs of hounds and learn to avoid the sounds of predator callers that have previously brought it into a close brush with danger.

It thus offers hunters a strong challenge under a variety of hunting conditions. Those who like to ride to the hounds, do so in pursuit of *reynard*. The less affluent hound hunter finds an equal chase for his dog. The game-caller, with his squealing rabbit or squeaking mouse call, electronic or mouth, can bring the red fox running

BELOW: The red fox is a clever animal that shows an almost unlimited ability to learn from its mistakes and "close calls." An individual will rarely make the same mistake twice.

day or night. And, the winter stalker, who is willing to follow the trail through the snow with his scoped rifle at the ready, can often get a shot at the fox asleep on a distant mound of snow.

No matter what the method of hunting chosen, the keen senses of the red fox must be taken into consideration at all times. An overhead or downwind and well-concealed vantage point is a must for any hunter who wants to score consistently.

The red fox is more often found in lightly wooded or open areas, including meadows and fields. Even when the animal is common in a given area, its nocturnal and shy nature may make observation difficult. The best times for fox-hunting are from late afternoon through the following early morning, although the canine may remain active longer on dark days.

It is a total opportunist in eating habits, able to make use of whatever it finds during daily travels. Berries, grapes, other fruits, nuts and grasses are used heavily when they are available, as are insects and other invertebrates. Small to medium animals and birds make up much of the winter diet.

For much of the time since European settlers began clearing the North American landscape, the red fox appears to have been expanding both its numbers and range into this newly-created prime habitat. However, the relatively recent spread of the coyote, with which it competes, into the East may be causing some problems for the red fox.

The red fox is found across the entire continent, north to south, except for the southwest corner of the United States and the northernmost reaches of Canada.

Gray fox

UROCYON CINEREOARGENTEUS

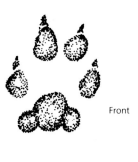

Front

Rear

Although there may be some overlapping of territories, in general red and gray foxes do not roam the same ranges. The gray tends to be more aggressive and intolerant of any competition. But, even more importantly, the two species prefer different habitats. While the red is a fox of the open fields and woodlands, the gray prefers the thick brushy tangles and deep forest. The gray also includes a great deal more fruit in its diet year-round, frequenting old orchards and wild grape tangles.

Adapted to the different habitat preference, all of the techniques of hunting that can be employed against the red will be equally effective on the gray. However, if the hunter takes to the chase, the gray fox will tire much more quickly

than the red. As the continent's only canine with any real tree-climbing ability, the gray fox often will tree up when it tires.

The gray fox leaves much more evidence of its presence in any area, because of its greater denning instinct. Whereas the red fox generally makes use of a den only during the breeding and pup-rearing period, the gray uses several dens within its home range with enough regularity to leave signs about them.

Adult gray foxes average six to 12 pounds in weight and as much as four feet in length, including a footlong tail. The animal is grizzled gray with reddish outlines, lower legs and feet. Its belly is white.

The range of the gray fox is more limited than that of the red. Except for extreme southeastern and southcentral Canada, the gray fox is a denizen of the US. It is largely absent from most of the Plains and the Rockies.

Canine Scat

LEFT: Unlike most members of the canine family, the gray fox is an able tree climber and will use this ability both as hunter and hunted.

Coyote
CANIS LATRANS

More eastern hunters become acquainted with the coyote each year, as the medium-sized canine expands its range to include new territories. By the late 1980s and early 1990s the line of advance, which is moving both east and south, had almost crossed all of Pennsylvania. Explanations for this are many and varied, but regardless of the real reason it appears that the traditional prairie wolf will soon be a resident of the entire United States, including Alaska, and all of southern Canada.

RIGHT: Although the coyote will take big game animals, and is rumored to kill many more than it actually does, it most often pursues much smaller species, particularly mice and voles.

LEFT: The coyote continues to expand its range and population, despite the best efforts of man to eradicate the species. It is currently moving into the mid-Atlantic states, after colonizing most of the rest of the continent.

FAR LEFT: A hunter fires at a swiftly approaching coyote, called in by the sound of a predator call.

Although the eastern coyote is considered a member of the same species as its western relations, it appears to have picked up some extra genetic material along its advance, possibly through crossbreeding with wolves. Where the western animal is usually about four feet in length and less than 35 pounds in weight, the new eastern coyote commonly exceeds both those maximums. The coat of the eastern animal also tends to be thicker than that of its western counterpart.

Wherever the coyote appears hunting seasons – if applied at all – are very liberal. Such is the fear that this animal strikes into the hearts of game management professionals. Man's best efforts through extensive hunting, trapping and poisoning have done little except cause the coyote population to boom. And there is some evidence, although still mostly circumstantial at this time, that the animal has had a negative impact on more preferred game species, such as white-tailed deer.

But the coyote is also gaining some new enthusiasts as it proves itself to be a cunning opponent. Hunters who have trailed the animal in both the West and the East believe the eastern version to be a tougher game animal, much less inclined to come dashing the minute the game caller begins to send out its call.

In the East, as many coyotes are probably shot through chance encounters with hunters in search of other game as by those specifically hunting the canines. For those few easterners who have viewed the animal as a sporting proposition, the hunt is primarily a matter of calling – generally with a squealing rabbit call – from a point of concealment. This method is also effective in the West.

In the West, however, the coyote is also hunted with hounds and by hunters on horseback or in four-wheel-drive vehicles, who cruise the animal's territory watching for their prey on the next ridge.

The coyote ranges from grizzled gray to reddish-brown, with buff to yellow belly and legs. The lower forelegs show a dark vertical line. The tail is black-tipped and bushy.

Timber wolf

CANIS LUPUS

Few animals on North America inspire the level of fear and respect that belongs to the timber, or gray, wolf. A single eerie howl is enough to stand the hair on end on the back of a hunter's neck, as he waits on stand for some other big game animal in the Canadian wild.

And yet, as cunning and powerful as this large canine may be, most tales of its prowess – particularly when directed against humans – are vastly exaggerated. Few wolf attacks have been documented against man in recent history, and many

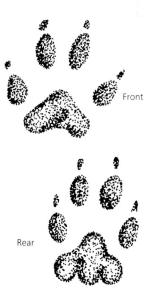

Front

Rear

of those from further in the past might be called into question as well. Even in areas where wolves are relatively common, a man might live for years without ever seeing more than their tracks and scat or hearing their howls. The modern timber wolf is well aware that its survival depends on avoiding man.

The timber wolf once claimed nearly the entire continent for its range, but today the animal is found in the wild only north of the Canadian-US border, except for limited populations in Califor-

nia, northern Minnesota, Wisconsin, Washington, Idaho and Montana. Although the animal remains legal game in Canada, few hunters pursue the wolf specifically.

The most recognized color coat on the timber wolf is grizzled gray, but an individual might be anything from black to white. All have a long, black-tipped, bushy tail. Most are less than six-and-a-half feet in length and 125 pounds in weight, but the largest on record tipped the scales at 175 pounds.

BELOW: The timber wolf has been among the most persecuted species of any in the animal kingdom. Today, however, even where the canine remains legal game, most hunters are satisfied with simply seeing one.

Chapter 9

BEAR

Black bear

URSUS AMERICANUS

Rear

Front

The black bear is the most widespread and abundant bear in North America, and becoming more so with each passing year. From the northern tree line in Canada and Alaska, south into Florida and Mexico, can all be considered the animal's range today, although forested areas with many openings are the preferred habitat.

This is a reclamation for the species, which inhabited this entire region commonly before the coming of the Europeans to the continent. From then on, it was hunted heavily for meat and fur and driven away by the clearing of the virgin forests. Much of the resurgence can be attributed to reintroduction and conservation efforts on the part of many state game agencies.

FACING PAGE: Under modern game management practices, the black bear has greatly expanded both its range and numbers.

RIGHT: The black bear occurs in many color variations, including a brown or chocolate phase (as shown), white and "blue." In some areas black with a white breast patch is common.

Bear Rump Roast

SERVES 3–4

2 garlic cloves

2–3 pound bear rump roast

fresh ground pepper and salt

beef bouillon

Flour and butter for roux

Cut garlic into small slivers and insert into gashes in roast. Season with pepper, and salt if desired. Roast uncovered at 325°F for 24 to 45 minutes per pound, with just enough beef bouillon to cover the bottom of the roasting pan. Baste frequently with the pan juices, adding more liquid if necessary. Make certain that the roast is well done – no pink in the center – before serving.

Make a gravy of the pan juices, thickening with a flour and butter roux as necessary. Serve over noodles.

(ELOISE GREE, NEW MEXICO WILDLIFE, ALAMOGORDIO DAILY NEWS)

In food habits, the black bear can be seen as little more than a living, moving garbage can. Anything edible that it chances on during its daily routine, natural or manmade – from berries to animal carcasses to the remnants of peanut butter in a jar at a landfill – becomes part of its diet. Depending upon food availability, the bruin's habits range from scavenger to predator.

However, under wild conditions beyond the influence of man and his easy pickin's, more than half – generally closer to three-quarters – of the bruin's diet consists of fruits, berries and other vegetable matter.

Over much of the black bear's range this catholic attitude towards edibles is the greatest cause of problems for the animal. Once a bear learns to equate humans with food – which it is quick to do when hand-outs are offered or garbage cans are readily available – it is well on its way to becoming a "problem bear" that needs to be trapped and moved elsewhere or eliminated.

Most black bears are no more than six feet in length, nose to tail, and less than 400 pounds in weight. However, both of those limits are breached quite regularly. A very few specimens of more than 800 pounds have been officially re-

corded. Weights taken from scales are the only truly accurate assessment of a bruin, as most observers tend to grossly overestimate what they've seen.

As large as they are, black bears tend to move through even the thickest tangles with a minimum of noise. More than one hunter has looked up from a momentary lapse in attention to find his quarry well within range, having heard not a single or leaf rustle to warn of its approach.

Bear Steak Marinade
SERVES 6–8

4–5 pounds bear loin steak

2 cups red wine

1 bay leaf

½ teaspoon thyme

½ teaspoon pepper

1 medium onion, diced

1 cup wine vinegar

2 tablespoons dried parsley

1 tablespoon salt

2 cloves garlic, pressed

3 tablespoons butter

Combine everything but steak, butter and 1 garlic clove. Place steak into the marinade and let stand in refrigerator for 24 hours. Remove the steak from marinade and wipe dry with paper towel.

Grill the steak over hot coals until well done – no pink in middle – basting with garlic butter made from the remaining garlic clove pressed and mashed into the butter.

Remove the steak to a hot platter and dust lightly with salt and pepper.

Wonderful served with Spanish rice and fresh spinach salad.

(ELOISE GREEN, NEW MEXICO WILDLIFE, ALAMOGORDIO DAILY NEWS)

"Black" is not really an appropriate name for this animal, so-called when cinnamon, beige, white, blue and white-blazed color phases were all considered separate species. However, we now know that these are all only phases of the same bruin. The species includes the surprising race of white black bears which inhabit a few British Columbia islands, and the blue phase known as glacier bears found along Alaska's Yakutat Bay.

Hunting methods are as varied as the color possibilities. In areas where baiting is permitted, hunters wait in tree stands over baits, ranging from fish to stale doughnuts. Hounds are popular in other regions, where the fleeing animal is pursued until it trees, makes a stand in some tangle or escapes. And, in those areas with more restrictive regulations, groups of hunters will band together to stage drives, attempting to push the animals into standing shooters. Lone hunters, or those in small groups, might position themselves along areas frequented by bears and wait for the animals to go through their daily routine or for other hunters to frighten the animals into their gun sights.

Although its eyesight has long been viewed as the black bear's weakest sense, new evidence suggests that the animal might be able to see much better than previously supposed. Its powerful nose and ears have never been called into question.

RIGHT: A hunter takes aim at a Pennsylvania black bear.

LEFT: Although black bears are common compared to North America's two other species of bruin, it can take many years of hunting for the animal before a hunter meets with success.

Black bears are not the true winterlong hibernators that we once thought them to be. Many in the southern extremes of their range will be active all year round. And, even in the northern areas, warm winter days may bring some of them out of the den.

Dens are not always – perhaps not even usually – the boulder-enclosed caves that is the common belief. Shallow depressions out in the open, culverts under roadways, crawl spaces under porches, hollow trees and mounds of leaves in the crooks of trees have all housed bears during their winter sleep.

There seems to be some truth to the persistent tales that the flesh of the bear will range in taste from sweet to foul and oily, depending upon the animal's diet. However, the author has never tasted any black bear meat that could be described as anything less than palatable. Thorough cooking is a must to insure against trichinosis.

Brown bear

URSUS ARCTOS

Like its much smaller cousin, the brown bear has been viewed as one species with many variations in only very recent times. The color variations, which range from black to blonde, and the great size diversity that early naturalists encountered, led them to classify each new variation as a distinct species. As many as 86 of these "species" were described at one point.

Today it is generally agreed that there are two races of brown bear in North America: the grizzly (*Ursus arctos horribilis*), which lives in the interior forests and rarely weighs more than 1,000 pounds (more commonly less than 700 pounds); and the Kodiak (*Ursus arctos middendorffi*), which is found along the coastal regions of British Columbia and Alaska and can weigh more than 1,800 pounds.

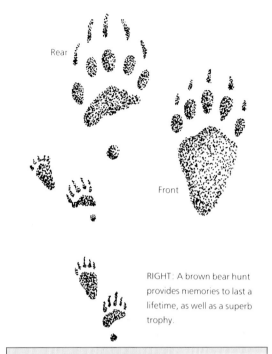

Rear

Front

RIGHT: A brown bear hunt provides memories to last a lifetime, as well as a superb trophy.

HUNTER'S HINTS

The brown bear is a great digger, seeking roots, bulbs, marmots and ground squirrels. In areas where marmots or ground squirrels are present, bear excavations are a sure sign of a good bear population.

Crockpot Bruin Stew

SERVES 6

2 pounds bear meat in cubes

margarine

6 carrots, sliced

2 large onions, cut into large chunks

3 stalks celery, sliced

1 pound stewed tomatoes

½ teaspoon whole cloves

2 bay leaves

6 garlic cloves, crushed

1 teaspoon onion powder

1 cup water

Sauté the meat in enough margarine until it is cooked completely through (no pink in middle). Mix with the remaining ingredients in a crockpot. Cook on high for 4 hours, and then on low for 8 more hours.

(THE AUTHOR)

RIGHT: The brown bear has a well-deserved reputation as the most dangerous animal on the North American continent. Today, however, it occupies such a limited range that extensive travel is required to put most people into close contact with the great bear.

Apart from a few scattered populations that number less than 1,000 total, mostly in national parks, the wild brown bear is gone from the lower 48 United States. Once the great bear roamed throughout the US, west and across the plains, and as far east as Ohio. But man has found its wide-ranging, lording lifestyle too much of a threat to himself and his livestock.

Also like its black bear relations, the brown bear can make a meal of virtually anything edible that it finds. But this much larger bruin is also a much more capable predator, regularly preying upon everything from salmon to moose.

Hunting brown bear is a nearly 100 per cent guided activity. This usually means glassing slopes, ridges, streams and the like which the guide knows the bear to frequent, until a suitable bruin is spottted. The shot may then be taken at considerable distance or after a stalk to gain some ground on the bear. Archery hunting for

bear has become increasingly popular over the years, necessitating a much closer approach to the prey.

Brown bears are similar to black bears in that they are not true hibernators and may rise from the dens in a particularly warm winter period. However, this is much more common among black bears. More often than not, the brown bear den will be a hole that it has dug or enlarged to just fit its body dimensions.

Polar bear

URSUS MARITIMUS

The polar bear is the ruler of the Arctic. It generally fears nothing that it encounters, and has been known to attack man.

Large and white is the only description needed to instantly identify this bruin. The great white bear of the North averages as much as 1,300 pounds in weight and measures up to 11 feet in length.

The overall impression is white, except for the black nose pad, lips and eyes – although yellowish individuals are not uncommon. The hollow hairs are actually clear, but appear white because they reflect light. This hollow nature allows the hairs to act as a solar heat collector, gathering ultraviolet radiation and conducting it to the bear's black skin beneath. The polar bear's fur also retains the heat extremely well, and provides a great deal of buoyancy in the water for this excellent and avid swimmer.

The senses of the polar bear are acute. Reports of bears being able to scent prey, such as seals, at a distance of 40 miles appear reliable.

Unlike the brown and black bears, the polar bear is almost entirely a meat-eater, be it carrion or the bear's own kill. Also unlike their more southerly relations, polar bears do not den for the winter. But females generally den to give birth to their young and any individual bear might seek refuge from particularly severe weather in a temporary shelter.

Other than native peoples of the North, few hunters today have the opportunity to hunt polar bears. This may usually only be done by buying into the kill allowed to the natives by the Canadian government.

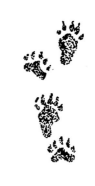

Front

Rear

BELOW: The white, hollow-centered fur of the polar bear acts much like a solar energy system, gathering heat from the sun and holding close to the animal's skin.

Chapter 10

FELINES

Mountain lion

FELIS CONCOLOR

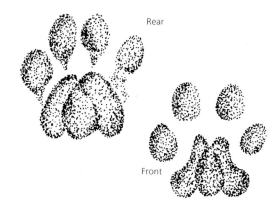

Rear

Front

Mountain-lion hunting ranks among the most controversial pursuits in today's hunting fraternity. Through court action last year, anti-hunting forces were able to challenge the annual hunt in California and eventually have it cancelled.

Elsewhere in several western states, however, North America's largest wild cat is still pursued. Chasing the cougar with hounds, a pursuit which may last for hours before the animal is treed or gives the dogs the slip, is the most common method. Hounds that show their proficiency in

BELOW : Although sightings of the big cat throughout the eastern half of the continent continue, except for a very small population in Florida the mountain lion is a creature of the West.

HUNTER'S HINTS

Although the mountain lion is one of the fastest animals on earth over a short distance, it soon runs out of steam. If your dog surprises a mountain lion, the cougar is likely to be panicked into full flight, and will bay or tree quite quickly.

tirelessly trailing mountain lions – all the while ignoring all other scent trails – are highly prized and generally owned only by professional guides.

The mountain lion ranges from six to nine feet in length, including a black-tipped tail that might extend three feet, and weighs from 75 to 275 pounds. It is yellow-brown to tawny with a white to buff belly. The head appears small relative to the body and the ears are small, round and erect.

It rarely reveals itself physically to man, but it does leave signs that the trained eye can discern. Sometimes circling vultures, crows and other carrion birds will reveal the spot where the cat hid a kill that was too large to eat in one sitting. Scratching posts – trees covered with scratches and gashes along their trunks – are usually found along the cat's regular trails. Fair amounts of scat, often showing bits of hair and bone, will generally be found along those same trails.

Under most circumstances, the cougar is a silent stalker. But it has a wide repertoire of calls, including a piercing scream that has been likened to that of a terrified girl.

Once ranging across the entire continent, except for the far north, the mountain lion today is confined primarily to the western half, British Columbia south through Texas. Small populations are also found in Louisiana, Tennessee and Florida. Reports of the big cat, generally refuted by game management agencies, persist in placing it in all states east of the Mississippi and even into Canada.

The cat's favored habitat has also diminished with the pressures brought by man's movements into the mountain lion's habitat. Adaptable to everything from semi-arid deserts to tropical forests, the mountain lion today keeps mostly to

mountainous areas. In relatively undisturbed regions, the cat remains active throughout the daylight hours, which is contrary to the habits of most wild cats.

ABOVE: The mountain lion prefers to feed exclusively on large animals, such as deer, because of the benefit of getting a lot of meat in a single kill. However, the cat will feed on everything down to mice and insects when deer are not abundant.

Bobcat

FELIS RUFUS

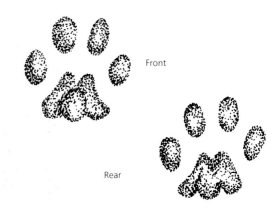

Front

Rear

The only wild cat in North America that appears to be expanding both its numbers and its range, the bobcat is finding its niche in mountainous, wild areas in the midst of man's habitations. It has always been the continent's most numerous cat, even during the days of government-sponsored mass extermination programs that numbered the bobcat among the varmints that should be done away with.

With the exception of several hundred square miles to the south and west of the Great Lakes region, nearly all of the United States and some areas of southern Canada are now home to this hardy feline.

A pack of hounds or a game call imitating a dying rabbit are about the only ways to see the bobcat in daylight, as it is an elusive and highly nocturnal animal. Even with these aids, early morning and late afternoon are generally the most productive times of day.

Prior knowledge of the cat's daytime hide-out, often on a protected ledge with a commanding view of some secluded valley, can be used to ambush the bobcat from some distance. But this is a method for taking only one or two cats per year, as it requires much scouting when the ground is covered with snow to locate and trail the animal through its haunts. It also involves a great deal of chance, as a single cat will have several such hide-outs, using each one only every few days and readily abandoning any where it senses the least threat.

About the only sign of its presence that the bob-

RIGHT: Bobcats are generally found in the wildest portions of their range; however, they have been able to adapt to fill the wild niches left between man's developments.

Feline Scat

cat allows, except for the hide-outs and tracks in the snow, is its screaming wail, which it lets loose more frequently during the mating season in spring.

Bobcats are generally reluctant to eat truly putrified meat. But when they happen to make a large kill, such as a white-tail deer, or find a freshly dead animal, they will cache it for future use. A well-concealed stand overlooking such a cache is often productive, given enough observation time.

As with many predators today, some conservation-minded hunters are no longer taking the hunt through to its previously ultimate conclusion. A treed cat or a cat called close enough for a frame-filling photograph has become the modern trophy for these individuals.

The bobcat is yellow-brown to gray-brown, with indistinct spots across its body and a white belly, throat and chin. Its namesake bob-tail is from three to six inches in length, circled by two or three black bars and a black tip. The face features broken black lines and wide cheeks.

It is a small cat, measuring only a bit more than four feet in length at most and weighing from 14 to 65 pounds.

Lynx

FELIS LYNX

FACING PAGE: A helicopter herds pronghorn antelope towards a capture net strung up by biologists. The capture is necessary in an ongoing study of the animals.

BELOW: The huge-footed lynx does not come under much hunting pressure in its far north habitat.

The lynx is more commonly trapped than hunted. Most of its habitat is extremely remote and inaccessible. It will tree much quicker than either the mountain lion or the bobcat when jumped unexpectedly. But the thick evergreen forests and deep snow drifts that it calls home, favor the slow-running cat in most chases.

The lynx resembles a larger, scruffier bobcat with less coloration variation. It is buff to yellow-brown with some grayish to black hairs. The two- to five-inch tail is black tipped, as are the long ear tufts. The large cheek ruffs are pale with some black bars, and form a beard under the chin. The paws are large and heavily furred. The cats range from 29 to 42 inches in length and 11 to 40 pounds in weight.

Never overly abundant, it still occurs across nearly all of Canada, except the northernmost reaches, and throughout Alaska. It is also found in northern New England, New York, the Midwest and the western states, and along the Rockies into Wyoming and Colorado.

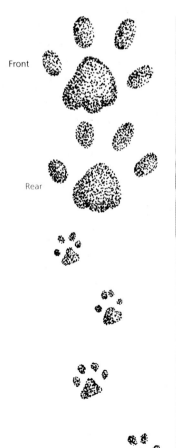

Front

Rear

Chapter 11

PRONGHORN
ANTELOPE

Pronghorn

ANTILOCAPRA AMERICANA

More commonly referred to as the pronghorn antelope or simply antelope, the pronghorn up close appears to be a spindly-legged, delicate creature. However, a herd of the medium-sized ruminants on the run offers quite a differ perspective, one of a graceful, able speedster.

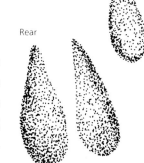

Rear   Front

BELOW: The pronghorn antelope is the only member of its family within the animal kingdom. It is the solitary remaining representative of a family that first arose nearly 20 million years ago.

Panhandle Pronghorn

SERVES 6

2 pounds of antelope, cubed

¼ to ½ cup flour, seasoned with black pepper

3 tablespoons bacon drippings

2 cups chopped onions

1–2 cups salsa or to taste

¼ teaspoon cumin

1 teaspoon chili powder

Dredge the meat in the seasoned flour. Spoon the drippings into large skillet and heat. Add the meat and brown on all sides. Remove the cubes from pan and reserve. Add the chopped onions and cook until golden. Return the meat to the pan and add all the remaining ingredients. Simmer 1½ hours or until the meat is tender. Serve over rice

(ELOISE GREEN, NEW MEXICO WILDLIFE, ALAMOGORDIO DAILY NEWS)

HUNTER'S HINTS

Before four-wheel drive vehicles became popular in hunting antelope, pronghorns headed for the shelter of the foothills when shooting started. Now they are more likely to find security on the big flats, where they can outmaneuver most things.

RIGHT: A pronghorn buck moves his small harem of does across a sage-covered hillside.

It is the fastest animal in North America, able to reach speeds of up to 70 miles per hour in short spurts and maintain 30 miles per hour over distances of almost 15 miles.

A creature of the open grasslands and sage-lands, the antelope has excellent vision through its large, protruding eyes and can pick up movement at several miles off. The animal also has able hearing, although in no way comparing to its eyesight. It takes very little to spook this animal over the ridge.

Because of its two extraordinarily keen senses, antelope-hunting is primarily a long-distance affair. The antelope are spotted in the distance, glassed for a nice trophy buck and then stalked to within shooting range of a hundred yards or so.

Another method, often employed by bow-hunters, is to hide in ambush at a waterhole that the antelope frequent. However, this is a pursuit for a patient hunter, as the antelope make their one daily trip to water at highly unpredictable times.

The pronghorn is tan to orange-brown across its back – about halfway down its side – down the outside of its legs, and across most of its neck. It is white from about halfway down its sides, across its chest and belly, the inner sides of its legs and its rump. There are also two white blazes across the throat. The buck also has a black band on each side of its snout and a black neck patch. An adult is from 50 to 60 inches in length and weighs between 75 and 140 pounds.

The buck also carries a pair of namesake pronged horns of 12 to 20 inches in length. The doe also has a pair of horns, although they usually

lack the pronged design and are less than four inches in length. The black sheath of keratin that encloses each horn is shed annually, but the horns continue to grow throughout the animal's life.

Early pioneers found immense numbers of antelopes roaming the Great Plains, but the subsequent development of their range has greatly reduced their numbers. Fencing of the open range alone accounted for the deaths of millions of the animals, which tend not to jump as avidly as they run. Early ranchers harbored deep resentment of

the animals – together with everything else that posed even an imaginary threat to their livestock – and shot and poisoned incredible numbers. The third blow against the animals came in the form of market hunting for meat and hides.

Today's numbers have stabilized with regulated hunting and are holding about level with the available habitat.

BELOW: The pronghorn antelope is a much sought-after trophy for many hunters. It is capable of speeds of more than 45 miles per hour and can run at 35 miles per hour for many miles.

Marinated Antelope

SERVES 6

3 pounds of shoulder, neck or breast meat

2 medium onions, sliced

1 carrot, sliced

2 stalks celery, chopped

1 clove garlic, crushed

1 cup water

½ cup salad oil

1 tablespoon ground peppercorn

1 tablespoon chopped parsley

1 bay leaf

Juice of 1 lemon

1 cup vinegar or wine

Remove skin, bones and tough tendons from meat and cut into 1½ inch pieces. Combine other ingredients in a large glass or stainless steel bowl, or in a large sealed plastic bag. Add the meat, stir to combine, and let stand in refrigerator for 1 to 2 days, turning the meat several times. Place meat and its marinade in large casserole and bring slowly to a boil. Cover and cook over low heat for 1½ to 2 hours or until the meat is tender. Remove the meat and strain the liquid, forcing vegetables through strainer. If desired, thicken the cooking liquid by stirring in a little flour made into a paste with some of the juice. Serve meat with sauce.

(ELOISE GREEN, NEW MEXICO WILDLIFE, ALAMOGORDIO DAILY NEWS)

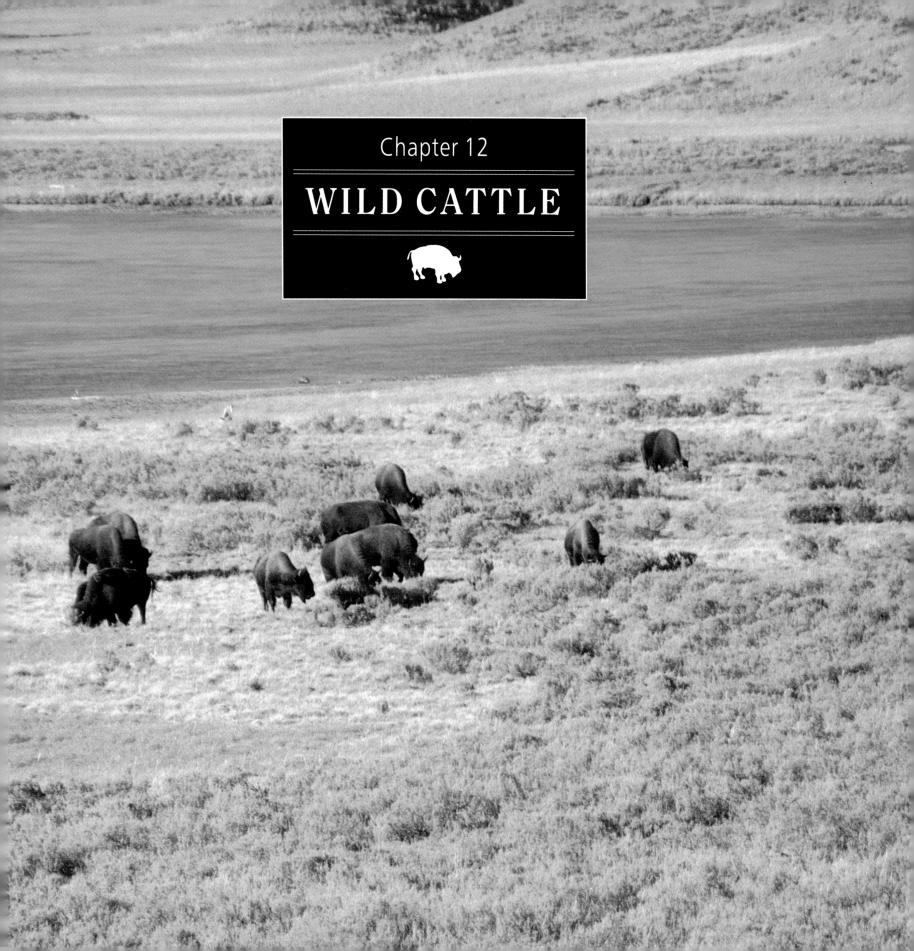

Chapter 12
WILD CATTLE

Bison

BISON BISON

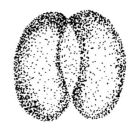

BELOW: The American bison is the symbol of the American West. It will never again roam the prairies by the millions as it once did, but the population has rebounded well under protection.

This great shaggy beast has been synonymous with the American West since the first Europeans laid eyes upon unbelievably large herds crossing the prairies. It is estimated to have once numbered 60 million head, spread from coast to coast. But the "white man's" persecution, which began in the 1830s, had reduced bison numbers to less than 1,000.

The animal seemed headed for extinction, when substantial conservation efforts finally got under way. But scattered herds were located and se-

Smith Summer Sausage

SERVES 8–12

4 pounds ground venison, elk, moose or bison, or a mixture

1 pound ground beef suet

2 tablespoons Morton's Tender-Quick Salt

2 tablespoons dry mustard

1 teaspoon mustard seed

2½ teaspoons garlic salt

2 tablespoons medium-grind black pepper

1 tablespoon whole peppercorns

2 tablespoons liquid smoke

1 teaspoon Worcestershire sauce

½ teaspoon seasoning salt

Mix all the ingredients thoroughly with hands. Cover and refrigerate for 2 days. Remove from the fridge, mix well again, cover and refrigerate for 2 more days. Take the meat out and mix well; form into 5 rolls or loaves. Place them on a rack in a baking pan and cook in a preheated 150°F oven for 8 hours, uncovered. These "sausages" freeze well.

(E THAYNE SMITH, FREELANCE TRAVEL AND OUTDOOR WRITER, WAGONER, OKLA.)

ABOVE: A herd of bison
grazes near a small river.

questered into national parks and national bison ranges in the United States, buffalo parks in Canada, and private ranges in both countries. The result is that more than 30,000 of the big animals are alive today.

One of the parks into which the last remaining free animals were shepherded was Yellowstone National Park, and there they have flourished. The northern herd gradually grew to about 1,000 head, and some animals began to migrate outside of the park for winter feeding.

First National Park Service hunters – and later Montana game wardens – shot the wandering animals. This was done to prevent the spread of brucellosis, which ranchers feared if the buffalo grazed on the winter ranges of domestic cattle.

Then, in 1985, legislation was passed in Montana that established the first public hunting of bison in North America – outside of private hunting preserves – in almost a century. Hunters, chosen by lottery, could cull those animals that crossed the man-made limits of the park.

The hunters killed only a few animals in each of the first few years of the public hunt. But in 1989, amid on-the-scene anti-hunting protests and national television coverage, harsh winter weather drove about 800 animals outside the park boundaries and hunters killed 569.

Admittedly there isn't much challenge to shooting the large, human-familiar animals at close range. However, it is a needed control of the herd that has shown its ability to quickly outgrow the available grazing lands inside the park. In addition, the hunters get a once-in-a-lifetime at a trophy and plenty of delicious meat.

Muskox

OVIBOS MOSCHATUS

The muskox is the shaggy-haired ox that roams the barren lands of northernmost Alaska and Canada in herds of as many as a hundred animals. Generally those herds are made up of cows and their offspring, with the adult bulls remaining solitary, except during the summer rutting season.

When threatened, the adults form a ring with their rumps touching and their well-armored heads facing outwards against the threat. The young are protected inside the circle. As effective as this defense may be against wolves, it is nothing in the face of a hunter with a rifle.

In former times, when the animal was hunted widely for meat and hides, the total population across North America became reduced to less than 500. However, more recently the numbers of muskox have climbed to an estimated 25,000, more than enough to sustain the limited and controlled sport-hunting targeted at them.

The muskox is dark brown across its body, covered in long shaggy hair that hangs almost to its feet. Its legs are white and it generally has some white along its saddle and on its forehead. It ranges from six to eight feet in length and weighs between 375 and 900 pounds. Both males and females have heavy, pointed horns.

LEFT: The muskox is not a widely sought-after big game animal, largely because the most difficult part of the hunt is reaching an area where a herd exists.

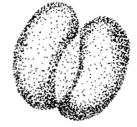

Chapter 13

WILD SHEEP AND GOATS

Bighorn sheep

OVIS CANADENSIS

Bighorns are found in regions not generally frequented by man – foothills at the base of steep rocky cliffs, high alpine meadows, arid desert areas are among the most likely sites – and, as a result, require the utmost of the hunter in search of a trophy.

Although the shot usually comes at only a couple of hundred yards, it is the long and careful stalk across rugged country that really gives the sport its rigorous reputation. Usually the stalk begins after the hunter and guide have watched the animals grazing and then going to rest, where they will remain for four to six hours.

The bighorn has excellent vision and can detect movement at nearly five miles. As for the beast's hearing, the slightest unnatural sound is picked up at much greater distances than most humans would think possible. Either clue can send the animals quickly out of sight.

Bighorn are fearless and able rock climbers, equipped with hooves that are soft and rubbery at their center but hard at the edges, to provide excellent traction. Sheer cliffs are no bar to this agile animal.

The rams of this species, which generally join the herds in winter, are well-known head-butters, whose clanging forehead crashes often reverberate for more than a mile through the mountains. Although such contests during the fall rutting season may last for many hours, just as often the size of the horns will decide status between the two competitors without a single blow being delivered. Only in rams of nearly equal size and temperament do the contests become necessary.

The meat of the animal is a genuine delicacy, and the horns have always been prized for their trophy value, even by the Indians. They have been recorded with spreads of 33 inches, and generally reach full curl – tip even with base – in the ram's seventh or eighth year.

The bighorn is five to six feet long and weighs from 120 to 190 pounds. In color it ranges from light tan in the desert portions of its range to dark brown in the northern mountains. The muzzle, the area around the eye, belly, backs of legs, and rump are white.

The sheep's range extends from southern British Columbia south into northern Mexico.

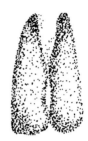

LEFT: A bighorn sheep has strong senses of sight and hearing. Something out of the ordinary picked up by either sense can send the animal quickly over the next ridge.

Dall sheep

OVIS DALLI

The dall sheep ranges from Alaska south through northern British Columbia and shares most of the same traits of the bighorn – if anything, it is even more wary. This species also tends to stick to smaller home ranges than the bighorn, both on a daily and seasonal basis. Hunting methods are similar to those employed for the bighorn, although more care is generally involved in taking a truly fine dall ram.

Dall ram horns are often longer than those of the bighorn, extending up to 48 inches in spread, but also are a bit more slender. Full-curl rams are less common than in the bighorn.

The dall sheep is about four-and-a-half to five-and-a-half feet long and weighs less than 200 pounds. In the northern portions of its range it is white, often with varying amounts of a yellowish-tint. In the southern-most extent, it is generally found in its dark gray phase, when it is known as "stone sheep." Between the two is found the Fannin or saddleback sheep, which is yet another phase of coloring in which the back or "saddle" is darker, while much of the rest of the sheep is white.

> **HUNTER'S HINTS**
>
> *Unlike bighorn sheep, Dall sheep usually bed near where they feed, often moving only from the grassy part of a slope to bed on a small rocky rise. This, combined with their pale coloring (which usually contrasts well with the environment), makes Dall sheep relatively easy to locate.*

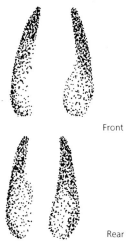

Front

Rear

LEFT: Long stalks and long shots are generally the rule for the hunter in search of a trophy dall sheep, the horns of which might sport a spread of as much as 48 inches.

Barbary sheep

AMMOTRAGUS LERVIA

An import from its native northern Africa, the Barbary sheep was introduced into the south-western United States in the 1950s. Scattered herds flourish there, and the sheep is hunted as a game animal.

It is four to six-and-a-half feet long and weighs 100 to 250 pounds. It is pale tan over most of its body, and paler or yellowish on its lower legs. A yellowish goat-like "beard" extends down along the throat.

Mountain goat

OREAMNOS AMERICANUS

A mountain goat hunt is not a thing of short duration. It generally begins with much horse-back-riding and climbing in rugged mountain

MOUNTAIN GOAT

LEFT: The mountain goat has never been a particularly abundant animal, but relatively light hunting pressure has not caused any downturn in the population.

country, stopping often to glass large expanses of the animal's mountainous home, well above the timberline. When a likely trophy is spotted, the next stage is to get above the animal, because the mountain goat expects danger to approach from below and generally escapes upwards.

The long, climbing stalk may put the hunter into position only to find that no shot can be taken. Often this is because a hit goat might be likely to plummet from its rocky crag and damage its horns. In addition, keen senses of vision, hearing and smell can help the animal to evade even the most assiduous hunter.

Because of these rigors the mountain goat has never come under the same hunting pressure as many more plentiful, lowland animals. This is for the best because the animal has never been a particularly abundant species. There are about as many alive today as there were before the coming of Europeans to North America.

The mountain goat is four to six feet long and weighs 45 to 140 pounds. It is white, often with a yellow tint. In winter the fur is long and shaggy, and the five-inch beard is retained year-round.

It ranges from southeastern Alaska south into northern Idaho, Montana and Washington.

Chapter 14
WILD SWINE

Javelina

DICOTYLES TAJACU

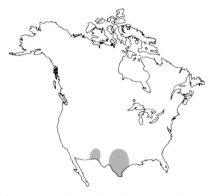

Also known as the collared peccary, the javelina occupies a limited range in the deserts and wastelands in the extreme southern reaches of Arizona and New Mexico and across much of Texas.

The small swine's range once extended several hundred miles further north, but its tasty meat and useful skin brought it under constant attack from early settlers in its territory. Fortunately for the javelina, man's coming was much harder on its few natural enemies, such as the jaguar and the cougar. Today the population has bounded to a more than adequate level to permit hunting.

Generally found in herds of five to 30, the javelina tends to inhabit a relatively small home area. A half-dozen square miles is a large range for all but the largest herds. The animal is most active from late afternoon through early the next morning, choosing to spend much of the hot daylight hours in a shallow soil bed or a cave.

Javelina Chops

SERVES 4–6

4–6 javelina chops

Flour seasoned with freshly ground
black pepper

vegetable oil

4–6 whole cloves

4–6 onion slices

4–6 red apple slices, unpeeled but
cored

water or apple cider

Dredge the chops in the seasoned flour. In a large skillet, heat oil and brown the chops on all sides. Into the center of each chop, place 1 whole clove, then top with 1 slice each of onion and apple. Pour a little water or cider into the bottom of the pan, cover and simmer for about 1 hour, until the meat is tender.

Buttered egg noodles or cornbread stuffing go well with this dish.

(ELOISE GREEN, NEW MEXICO WILDLIFE,
ALAMOGORDIO DAILY NEWS)

FACING PAGE: The javelina has few remaining natural enemies, other than man, and its population has been rebounding in recent years.

LEFT: A small herd of javelina move through a cactus-covered draw. Hunting for the animals often involves shots from considerable distances, although archers do take their share.

Wild boar

SUS SCROFA

A native of the Old World, wild boars have come to the wilds of North America in one of two ways: Wild stock from Europe or Asia stocked as big game for hunting; or escaped domesticated stock which established a feral population.

The first recorded intentional stocking took place in 1893, when about 50 wild-stock animals from Germany were released on a hunting preserve in New Hampshire. However, these were probably not the first wild boar to roam North America. Significant numbers had been escaping from domestication throughout the New World since the first European settlers established their farms hundreds of years earlier.

Except for the purebred wild boars on a few enclosed hunting preserves, most of today's population in the wild is either the result of crossbreeding between pure European boars and domestic hogs gone feral, or the straight line of descent from feral domestic hogs. All are of the same species as our domestic hogs.

However, the wild boar is instantly recognizable as something other than domestic. It is a shaggy-haired, grizzled animal, with a heavy mane about its neck and shoulders and along its

Such cave areas and the trails that lead to them – often detectable by the thick musky odor that the javelina leaves – are prime ambush locations. Thickly brushed gullies and draws also are frequented by the animal as it feeds.

Although most shots at javelina are taken at a few hundred yards, other hunters pursue them with handguns. This requires a much closer approach for their shooting.

Some hunters tell of the ferocity of the javelina, however, such instances seem to be the exception rather than the norm. What appears to be a charge may, in fact, be attributed to the animal running mistakenly toward a threat that its relatively poor eyesight failed to detect. A cornered or wounded javelina may present a different situation entirely and is well-armed for a fight .

When frightened the animal can run as fast as 25 miles per hour, but will generally do so for only a short distance. The herd will scatter, rejoining one another after the threat can no longer be detected.

About three to three-and-a-half feet long and weighing from 35 to 70 pounds, the javelina is grizzled gray to black across much of its body, with a lighter curved band from back to cheek on each side, a similarly lighter outline on the ear-tips and a brownish tint at the cheeks. It also has a bristly appearance across most of its body, particularly noticeable along the back. It has a pig-like snout, on each side of which the short, sharp tusks protrude both upwards and down.

ABOVE: The wild boar can be a dangerous big game animal, often armed with tusks that can rip open a chasing hound or hunter.

RIGHT: Hunters gather around a trophy wild boar downed by one of their party.

Small herds of five or six is the norm, but groups of several dozen have been reported. In areas where the favored nut trees give ample crops, the animals might inhabit a range of less than 10 square miles. But under less favorable conditions that range might expand to 60 square miles.

The wild boar in North America has almost no natural enemies other than man, and as a result its numbers can expand quickly. Some states – where the animal has become a real nuisance on agricultural crops – have no closed season on the wild boar at all.

Hunting is often accomplished with the help of a pack of hounds. Ambush hunting is not often effective, since the boars tend to follow no set trails as might a white-tailed buck.

The wild boar is a tough animal. It can continue a charge even after sustaining a wound that will eventually kill it. Dogs are often killed and maimed by a cornered boar, as have some unlucky hunters.

back. Often it exhibits long protruding tusks, both upper and lower. The upper tusks might be as long as nine inches, although the average is less than six. The color of the purebred wild boar is black, brown or gray. The much more common "mongrel" boars may also be reddish, tan or spotted.

It can be a huge animal, measuring from four to six feet and weighing from 80 to 450 pounds.

The wild boar is primarily an animal of the southeastern United States, west into Texas. However, feral hogs have recently gained much attention as nuisance animals in California. In addition, many hunting preserves across the United States maintain populations of the animal.

Chapter 15

MISCELLANEOUS
SPECIES

The last few species that make up this chapter are often overlooked by books on hunting. They are considered too much of a novelty, or not of interest to enough hunters. However, in our attempt to present a comprehensive picture of the North American hunting scene, we would be remiss not to include some small mention.

ABOVE: The bullfrog provides excellent sport for an archery or small arms hunter, as well as the delicacy of frog's legs.

Bullfrog
RANA CATESBEIANA

More commonly viewed as a summertime pursuit for young children, the bullfrog can actually provide ample bow-and-arrow sport. In addition there is the added bonus of delicacy-level table fare that frog's legs have become. In regions where it is hunted regularly, this largest of North America's frogs has become downright wary.

In areas where lights are permitted in the pursuit of the hopper, most hunting is a simple matter of moving out on the lake, river or swamp at night with a bright beam to temporarily "freeze" the bullfrog while it is scooped up by hand.

But a daytime stalking method along the same type habitat provides greater sport for the archer. The target is small and the shot usually must be taken at least over several yards.

The bullfrog is from four to nine inches in length and might weigh as much as a half-pound. It is green to yellow-brown above, with some darker mottling, and white to light yellow on its belly. The large external eardrum is circular and generally darker than the rest of the frog.

Nine-banded armadillo
DASYPUS NOVEMCINCTUS

While the armadillo, with its habit of hiding inside its armor plating, cannot truly be considered a game animal, it is hunted regularly enough in some southern states to warrant a mention. But hunting for this strange animal is generally done with a club rather than a gun or bow, and for the rich meat rather than for any sporting purpose.

American alligator
ALLIGATOR MISSISSIPPIENSIS

Until recently, the alligator was considered an endangered species. But under strict protection it came back, until game agencies in a few southern states deemed there to be enough of the reptiles to warrant limited hunts. Florida, for example, issued 228 permits in 1989 and 189 in

1990. Each permittee was required to undergo a six-hour training course before being allowed to take up to 15 alligators of four feet or longer.

The alligator is the largest reptile in North America. Adults range from six to 19 feet in length. They are generally dark gray or pale black, losing the lighter crossbands that they had as juveniles. Their backs and tails are distinctly layered in "toothy" sections.

BELOW: The carp is a large fish that can provide a lot of fight on the end of a line. Its flesh is generally considered inedible, although this is not at all true.

RIGHT: Alligators have rebounded so well under strict protection that limited hunting is now permitted in some areas.

Roughfish

Across North America there are approximately 270 species of carp, suckers and minnows, of which many larger species are hunted with bow and arrow. This is generally accomplished by a wading archer, or one riding in the bow of a small boat over shallow water. A specialized bow-fishing rig is generally employed. This attaches some sort of reel to the bow, and a heavy line to the arrow, for the retrieval of the fish.

Chapter 16

OUTFITTERS
& TAXIDERMISTS

There are two groups of professionals who can make your hunting experiences infinitely more enjoyable: the outfitter, during the hunt itself, and the taxidermist, in the years to follow. Though care must be exercised in choosing either, the vast majority – as a matter of fact everyone I've met from these two professions – are highly skilled and conscientious professionals.

But there is room for the quick-buck scam artist, or the well-intentioned but not so capable individual, to slip into the ranks. Frustrating tales of poor accommodation and lack of game are not difficult to find, although many I've heard strike me as being more the hunter's fault than the outfitter's. The key rule for the hunter who is preparing to place several hundred, if not thousands, of dollars into an outfitter's hands is to give a thorough review to the reputation and visible work of that person.

Ask other hunters, whose opinions you respect, about outfitters and taxidermists. For example, I never hesitate to recommend Pavillon Wapus Inc in Quebec for black-bear hunting or for walleye and northern pike fishing. I've had nothing but the very best of experiences and accommodations there. My brother feels the same way about Le Domaine Shannon Inc, also in Quebec, and for the same reasons. Similarly, we each have taxidermists with whose work we are both familiar and pleased.

RIGHT: A well-done taxidermy mount, like this trophy whitetail buck, should appear lifelike and natural in every sense of the words.

Ask to see photos that other hunters may have taken during their trips. Although they will usually focus on the hunter with his trophy, background scenes might give a feel for the condition of the equipment and lodging that the outfitter offers. The large sports and outdoor shows held each winter across the country offer similar opportunities. The outfitter booths are generally well stocked with photos of successful sportsmen.

In addition, spend time talking in depth with any outfitter you're considering. If you've "studied up" on the subject, you might be able to assess how knowledgeable he is on the trophy you want to pursue. You might also form an opinion on whether he is the type of individual with whom you could be comfortable.

Another source of information about guides and outfitters are state and provincial game agencies. Most public agencies, however, are reluctant to report anything negative about their own areas. The information from these sources typically ranges from a simple photocopied list of names, addresses and telephone numbers to well-prepared books that even rate the accommodations.

As for taxidermists, other hunters can provide some information, but it is actually better to examine their work in person.

Watch for the following items in each mount you inspect; these are the criteria that the few taxidermy schools across the country use in grading their students:

● Anatomical accuracy. Does the structure of the head and body (if a full-body mount) appear natural? Do the muscles look like the muscles of similar animals you've seen in the wild? Are the neck, all limbs and tail in natural positions? Do the eyes and mouth look alive?

● Natural coloration. Does anything about the color of the mount strike you as odd? Why?

● Symmetry. Do both sides of the mount have a similar appearance? Or do they look like they may have come from two different animals?

● Overall craftsmanship. Does the fine detail work hold up under close inspection? Has the taxidermist taken great pains with the smallest of lines?

Inspect the taxidermist's show pieces at close range – and from a distance – with all of these criteria in mind. In addition, ask the taxidermist about his training, background, awards for his work and certification/licensing. There are professional schools that specialize in this career path. Most states and provinces require taxidermists to complete testing to obtain certification or licensing.

LEFT: Skillful taxidermists take great pains in recreating the animal that the hunter brought to them to preserve as a memory of his hunt.

Chapter 17

TEACHING A CHILD TO HUNT

Even before the baby takes its first steps, many a hunter begins dreaming of the day when he can pass on his outdoor heritage to his new son or daughter. And while that may be a bit early to start, a true conservation-minded hunter's training often begins well before he or she is old enough to legally hunt.

Respect for the outdoors and the animals that live there – the real basis of hunting – can be planted as soon as the child is old enough to grasp the most basic concepts, such as a rabbit's ability to run fast or a squirrel's agility in climbing a tree. The "teacher" must see the world through the "student's" eyes and translate everything possible to that level. Concepts that can't make the jump should wait for later.

Unhurried, unfocused trips into the forest or the field should be frequent, with the interest of the child leading the way. Forget the customary paths – perhaps the adult can pick up something new as well.

TOP RIGHT: A father and son take part in the ritual of hunting that has been passed from generation to generation for thousands of years.

RIGHT: Hunter safety classes are held across the country to prepare first-time hunters to enjoy their sport safely.

The first hunting trips should come years before the youngster may carry his own weapon. Generally they should be spent in the pursuit of easier game that is abundant enough to offer somewhat steady action and at least some measure of success.

These trips should be filled with excitement and joy. All worries and bothers – from the outside world or that may occur during the outing itself – should be minimized and quickly left in the dust.

A few years before legal hunting age, the child should be given his or her first gun, an air rifle. Ground rules, such as never loading or firing the gun unless under the supervision of an adult, should come *with* the gun rather than arise with various situations along the way.

Target practice should include both the backyard or range, and later perhaps a "course" of tin cans laid out by the adult through a woodlot to simulate hunting situations. The child's handling of the gun should be observed throughout this period and any irresponsible actions should be corrected gently and with guidance, rather than in a nagging fashion.

As hunting age approaches, hunter-safety or hunter-education – in the formalized setting offered by state game agencies and sportsmen's clubs – is the next logical step.

The Christmas before the child's first year of real hunting is often the time for an advance to the first weapon of a higher degree. A single-barrel, break-action, 20-gauge shotgun is a fine first choice, giving the child the fire power to take his or her first small game, as well as later, larger game, like the whitetail deer. Many sessions of informal clay-pigeon shooting should fill the months between that Yuletide and the first day of hunting. Again any irresponsible actions must be headed off quickly but sensitively.

When that fateful first day arrives, perhaps the adult should leave his own gun at home and instead concentrate on making the child's outing something that will stick favorably in both their minds for many years to come.

The young hunter should not be pushed beyond his capabilities. A few hours of waiting in ambush for squirrels may be all he or she can handle that first trip. Stamina will grow with each new outing and the freedom to be a bit farther away from

the adult can be increased gradually.

In the second or third year of hunting, the youngster will probably show himself ready to handle a more powerful weapon, such as a 12-gauge shotgun or that first deer rifle. Again, either of these are traditional Christmas gifts in a hunting household.

Throughout this entire period, lessons in respect for the wild creatures and in understanding their lives and habits should continue. The goal is the true sportsman-hunter, who can return home at the end of the day afield with an empty game bag but a heart and head filled with the wonderment and excitement of the outdoors.

RIGHT: Hunting today is truly a family sport. Here a father, his son and his daughter are enjoying a day afield together.

LEFT: Part of each hunter safety course involves shooting, both to test the young hunter's marksmanship and his or her handling of the firearm.

Appendix I:

GAME AGENCIES

United States

Dept. of Conservation &
Natural Resources
64 N. Union St
Montgomery, AL 36130

Dept. of Fish & Game
P.O. Box 3–2000
Juneau, AK 99802

Game & Fish Dept.
2222 W. Greenway Rd
Phoenix, AZ 85023

Game & Fish
Commission
#2 Natural Resources
Dr.
Little Rock, AR 72205

Dept. of Fish & Game
1416 Ninth St
Sacramento, CA 95814

Dept. of Natural
Resources
Division of Wildlife
6060 Broadway
Denver, CO 80216

Dept. of Environmental
Protection
State Office Building
165 Capitol Ave
Hartford. CT 06106

Dept. of Natural
Resources &
Environmental Control
Division of Fish &
Wildlife
P.O. Box 1401
Dover, DE 19903

Game and Fish
Commission
620 S. Meridian St
Tallahassee
FL, 323399–1600

Dept. of Natural
Resources
Floyd Towers East
205 Butlet St
Atlanta, GA 30334

Dept. of Land & Natural
Resources
Division of Forestry and
Wildlife
1151 Punchbowl St
Honolulu, HI 96813

Fish & Game Dept.
600 S. Walnut
Box 25
Boise, ID 83707

Dept. of Conservation
Lincoln Tower Plaza
524 S. Second St
Springfield, IL 62706

Dept. of Natural
Resources
Office Building 608 St
Indianapolis, IN 46204

Dept. of Natural
Resources
E. Ninth and Grand Ave
Des Moines,
IA 50319–0034

Dept. of Wildlife & Parks
900 Jackson St
Suite 502
Topeka, KS 66612–1220

Dept. of Fish & Wildlife
#1 Game Farm Rd
Frankfurt, KY 40601

Dept. of Wildlife and
Fisheries
P.O. Box 15570
Baton Rouge, LA 70895

Dept. of Inland
Fisheries & Wildlife
284 State St
Station #41
Augusta, ME 04333

Dept. of Natural
Resources
Tawes State Office Bldg
Annapolis, MD 21401

Dept. of Fisheries,
Wildlife &
Environmental Law
100 Cambridge St
Boston, MA 02202

Dept. of Natural
Resources
Box 30028
Lansing, MI 48909

Dept. of Natural
Resources
500 Lafayette Road
St Paul, MN 55155

Dept. of Wildlife
Conservation
Southport Mall
P.O. Box 451
Jackson, MS 39205

Dept. of Natural
Resources
P.O. Box 176
Jefferson City,
MO 65102

Dept. of Fish, Wildlife
and Parks
1420 East Sixth
Helena, MT 59620

Game & Parks
Commission
2200 N. 33rd St
P.O. Box 30370
Lincoln, NE 68503

Dept. of Wildlife
Box 10678
Reno, NV 89557

Fish & Game Dept.
34 Bridge St
Concord, NH 03301

Division of Fish, Game
and Wildlife
CN 400
Trenton, NJ 08620

Game and Fish Dept.
Villagra Building
Santa Fe, NM 87503

Division of Fish and
Wildlife
Dept. of Environmental
Conservation
50 Wold Road
Albany, NY 12233

Wildlife Resources
Commission
Archdale Building
512 N. Salisbury
Raleigh, NC 27611

Game and Fish Dept.
100 N. Bismarck
Expressway
Bismarck, ND 58501

Dept. of Natural
Resources
Fountain Square
Columbus, OH 43224

Dept. of Wildlife
Conservation
1801 N. Lincoln
Oklahoma City,
OK 73152

Dept. of Fish and
Wildlife
107 20th St
La Grande, OR 97850

Game Commission
P.O. Box 1567
Harrisburg,
PA 17105–1567

Dept. of Environmental
Management
9 Hayes St
Providence, RI 02903

Wildlife and Marine
Resources
Rembert C. Dennis
Building
P.O. Box 167
Columbia, SC 29202

Game, Fish and Parks
Dept.
445 East Capitol
Pierre, SD 57501–3185

Parks & Wildlife Dept.
4200 Smith School Rd
Austin, TX 78744

Wildlife Resources
Agency
P.O. Box 40747
Ellington, TN 37204

Division of Wildlife
Reserves
Dept. of Natural
Resources
1596 W. North Temple
Salt Lake City,
UT 84116–3156

Dept. of Fish and
Wildlife
Waterbury Complex
10 South Waterbury,
VT 05602

Dept. of Game & Inland
Fisheries
4010 W. Broad St
Box 11104
Richmond, VA 23230

Dept. of Wildlife
600 N. Capitol Way
Olympia, WA 98504

Dept. of Natural
Resources
1800 Washington St E
Charleston, WV 25305

Dept. of Natural
Resources
Box 7921
Madison, WI 53707

Game & Fish Dept.
Cheyenne, WY 82002

Canada

Fish & Wildlife
Main Floor, North Tower
Petroleum Plaza
9945–108 St Edmonton
Alta. T5K 2G6

Ministry of Environment
and Parks
Parliament Buildings
Victoria, BC V8V 1X5

Dept. of Natural Resources
Legislative Building
Winnipeg, Man. R3C 0V8

Dept. of Natural Resources
P.O. Box 6000
Fredericton,
New Brunswick E3B 5H1

Wildlife Division
Building 810
Pleasantville
P.O. Box 4750
St. John's,
Newfoundland A1C 5T7

Dept. of Renewable
Resources
Government of the NWT
Yellowknife
NWT X1A 2L9

Dept. of Lands and
Forests
P.O. Box 698
Halifax, Nova Scotia
B3J 2T9

Ministry of Natural
Resources
Toronto,
Ontario M7A 1W3

Canadian Wildlife Service
Agriculture Canada
Ottawa K1A 0C5

Dept. of Community and
Cultural Affairs
P.O. Box 2000
Charlettetown
PE1 C1A 7N8

Dept. of Recreation, Fish
and Game
Place de la Capitale 150 East
St-Cyrille Blvd.
Quebec City,
Quebec G1R 2B2

Dept. of Parks and
Renewable Resources
3211 Albert St
Regina,
Saskatchewan S4S 5W6

Dept. of Renewable
Resources
Box 2703
Whitehorse,
Yukon Terr Y1A 2C6

Appendix II:

HUNTING ORGANIZATIONS

Safari Club International
4800 W. Gates Pass Road
Tucson, AZ 85745

National Shooting Sports Foundation Inc.
555 Danbury Road
Wilton, CT 06897

International Association of Fish and Wildlife
Agencies
444 North Capitol St N.W.
Suite 534
Washington, DC 20001

International Shooting and Hunting Alliance
1825 K St
Suite 901
Washington, DC 20006

National Rifle Association
1600 Rhode Island Ave N.W.
Washington, DC 20036

Quail Unlimited Inc.
P.O. Box 10041
Augusta, GA 30903

Ducks Unlimited Inc.
1 Waterfowl Way at Gilmer Road
Long Grove, IL 60047–0216

National Muzzle Loading Rifle Association
P.O. Box 67
Friendship, IN 47021

Pheasants Forever Inc.
P.O. Box 75473
St. Paul, MN 55175

Prairie Grouse Technical Council
University of Minnesota
Natural Resources Department
Crookston, MN 56716

Rocky Mountain Elk Foundation
P.O. Box 8249
Missoula, MT 59807

The Canvasback Society
P.O. Box 101
Gates Mills, OH 44040

Wildlife Legislative Fund of America
50 W. Broad St
Columbus, OH 43215

Ruffed Grouse Society
1400 Lee Drive
Coraopolis, PA 15108

National Wild Turkey Federation
770 Augusta Road
P.O. Box 530
Edgefield, SC 29824–0530

Game Conservation International
P.O. Box 17444
San Antonio, TX 78217

Boone and Crockett Club
241 S. Fraley Blvd.
Dumfries, VA 22026

Izaak Walton League
1401 Wilson Blvd. Level B
Arlington, VA 22209

Foundation for North American Wild Sheep
720 Allen Ave.
Cody, WY 82414

Whitetails Unlimited Inc.
P.O. Box 422
Sturgeon Bay, WI 54235

Appendix III:

ADDITIONAL READING

Bland, Dwain, *Turkey Hunter's Digest* (DBI 1986).

Brister, Bob, *Shotgunning: The Art and the Science* (Winchester Press 1976).

Cadieux, Charles, *Goose Hunting* (Stoeger Publishing Company 1983).

Carlisle, G.L., *Grouse and Gun* (Century Hutchinson 1988).

Coles, Charles, *Shooting and Stalking: A Basic Guide* (Century Hutchinson 1988).

Darner, Kirt I., *Hunting the Rockies – Home of the Giants* (Darner Books 1988).

Douglas, James, *The Sporting Gun* (David & Charles 1983).

Duffey, David M., *Bird Hunting Tactics* (Willow Creek Press 1989).

Ellman, Robert (ed.), *All About Deer Hunting in America* (Winchester Press 1976).

Fergus, Charles et al, *Rabbit Hunting* (Allegheny Press 1985).

Geer, Galen, *Meat on the Table: Modern Small-Game Hunting* (Paladin Press 1985).

Gilchrist, Duncan, *The Big Game Hunter's and Fisherman's Complete Guide to Field Care of Trophies* (Stoneydale Press Publishing 1986).

Helgeland, Glenn, *Complete Bow Hunting* (North American Hunting Club 1987).

Hunter's Guide to Professional Outfitters (Safari Press 1988).

Janes, E.C., *Ringneck! Pheasants and Pheasant Hunting* (Crown Publishing 1975).

Kinton, Tony, *The Beginning Bowhunter* (ICS Books 1985).

Laubach, Don and Henckel, Mark, *The Elk Hunter* (Falcon Press 1989).

Meyer, Jerry, *Bear Hunting* (Stackpole 1983).

Pyle, Wilf E., *Hunting Predators* (Stoeger Publishing Co. 1985).

Shelsby, Earl and Gilford, James (eds), *Basic Hunter's Guide* (National Rifle Association 1982).

Strung, Norman, *The Art of Hunting* (Cy De Cosse 1984).

Taylor, Buck, *Turkey Hunting: Spring and Fall* (Outdoor Skills 1983).

Whelen, Townsend, *Hunting Big Game* (Wolfe Publishing Co.).

INDEX

CREDITS

t = top; b = bottom; l = left; r = right.

Doe Anderson/Mossberg: pages 11 l, 12 br, 13 tl.
Hank Andrews: page 126, 139.
Joel Arrington: pages 7 t, 76, 99 l, 100 b.
Jill Barnes: pages 67 b, 89 t.
L. L. Bean Inc.: pages 20 t, 20 b, 21 t.
Mike Blair: pages 59 r, 123.
Browning: pages 10 b, 11 l, 12 l, 13 tr, 14 lb t, 15 bl, 17 t.
Richard Day: pages 35, 47, 63, 117 r, 119 l.
Lane Eskew: pages 17 b, 33, 17 l t.
B. L. Fegely: pages 36, 83 b, 137, 150.
Tom Fegely: pages 6, 19, 22, 162 b, 169, 170 b, 171 b.
Pat Gerlach: pages 106 t, 108 r, 110 bl, 138.
Scott Wm. Hanrahan: pages 26 b, 148, 166, 167, 168.
Lorraine Harrison: track illustrations throughout.
Carol Herndon: page 83.
Tom Huggler: pages 38, 53, 58, 74 l, 77, 80 t, 81, 95 t.
Ken Hunter: pages 40, 136.
Clifford L. Jacobson: page 154.
Bob Lollo: page 84 b, 97 l, 118, 152.
Danny MacBride (illustrations): pages 10 t, 11 r, 13 b, 18 t, 27 r, 30.
Steve Maslowski: pages 8 b, 26 t, 42, 68, 70 t, 82, 102 l, 105 r, 129, 130 r, 158, 159, 163, 170 t.
Dick Mermon: pages 24 b, 46, 70 b, 85, 87, 91 t, 91 br, 96, 98, 100 t.
Neal and Mary Jane Mishler: pages 29, 59 t, 62, 64, 65, 134, 142.
Photri: pages 24 t, 25, 27 l, 28, 37, 41, 52 r, 56, 57, 73, 74, 84 t, 92 r, 93 r, 97 r, 100 t, 103 r, 105 l, 108 l, 109 b, 111, 112, 113, 115 l, 120 t, 125, 127, 132, 140, 145, 146, 155, 156, 157, 161, 162 t.
Quarto Publishing Ltd (photographer Ian Howes): pages 12 tr, 16 t, 16 b, 18 r, 18 b.
Marcus Schneck: pages 9 t, 21 l, 32, 34, 43 b, 44 t, 51 t, 66, 69 l, 92 l, 131, 141, 143, 149, 151, 153.
Gregory K. Scott: pages 15 br, 44 b, 59 b, 86, 101 b, 102 r, 103 l, 104 t, 106 b, 109 t, 110 t, 114 t, 114 b, 117 l, 120 b, 121.
Norm Smith: pages 23, 31, 54, 79, 80 b, 88, 94, 104 b, 107, 147.
Keith Sutton: pages 8 t, 21 br, 43 t, 49, 50, 51 b, 56, 67 t, 71, 75 r, 89 b.
Tom Tietz: pages 61, 78, 110 br, 160.
John Trout Jr: pages 124, 135.
Unicorn Stock Photos/J. Bisley: page 45.
Unicorn Stock Photos/Richard B. Dippold: page 119 r.
Unicorn Stock Photos/John Ebeling: pages 130 l, 165 b.
Unicorn Stock Photos/Christian Mundt: page 122.
Scott Weidensaul: pages 7 b, 9 b, 48, 72, 90, 91 bl, 93 l, 95 b, 115 r, 116, 133, 164, 165 t.
Gerald L. Wickkund: page 99 r.